365 Days of Classroom Fun

Early Childhood Development Activities &
Supply Lists for Every Day of the Year

Written by Kristen Ortwerth & Angela Feathers
Illustrations by Natalia Scabuso

<u>**FOREWORD**</u>

As a child, I spent time in multiple daycare settings (some better than others), and even in the earliest years of elementary & preschool, my very best memories are the ones that involved simple, DIY celebrations of even the most trivial things to help me remember books, animals, foods, historical events, scientific discoveries, and new cultures.

Little did I realize how hard my teachers must have worked behind the scenes to make those memories happen for me.

Our early childhood educators are overworked, underpaid, and (in some cases) massively undervalued. Lesson planning is critical to your success as an educator, but it can also be a royal pain, especially when you're just starting out in the field. When I set out to create this book, I had exactly that in mind: help early educators with ideas for their lesson plans that incorporate the concept of celebration & play into the classroom learning environment.

So many of my friends are educators, and they all have the same thing to say: executing your lesson plan well and seeing the joy light up all of those little faces is incredibly rewarding, but the thought of trying to come up with that many ideas and build a calendar out of them is exhausting. It's usually one of the things that they procrastinate most and force themselves into doing.

So, I wanted to help kickstart that creativity and inject a little bit of fun into lesson planning with a cheat sheet of ideas you can use to fill out your lesson plans for any day of the year. In this book, you'll find 365 days of reusable ideas for activities that incorporate educational play & celebration in early years educational environments. Each day's activity is tied to a national (USA) observance day or month. Some are serious or historical topics, some are simply interesting, and some of are very, very silly.

Take these ideas to turn your classroom into a celebratory learning lab that can help students to learn real world information though fun, engaging activities. I tried to pick holidays that recur on the same date every year so that you can reuse the ideas year over year. My goal in creating this book was to provide you with a resource you can use to reach any number of educational goals through memorable, engaging lessons without reinventing the wheel every time you sit down to do lesson planning!

My personal experience in a daycare setting notwithstanding, research studies prove that (at any age) when we are engaged and having fun while learning, our brains release a chemical called dopamine that can act as the brain's reward mechanism. In fact, dopamine in children goes beyond just reinforcing the joy of learning. Whenever it's released, we are far more likely to remember that experience; when it's not there, we have a much harder time retaining information.

This is the reason that incorporating play into learning is so very effective! Creating these types of activities and engaging events for our students is imperative to helping these minds grow and understand the things they need in ways that are positive and healthy.

Another major benefit of aligning your classroom activities to broadly recognized events is that it allows you to connect what's happening in the classroom to the real world, including with parents and others at home. It's a great idea to include these activities in weekly or monthly newsletters in addition to your daily sheets so that parents have easy insight to something their child is learning and working on in school. It gives them something charming and relatable that they can discuss at home.

Learners who connect information to their world helps them to understand its importance and relevance. Through these creative activities, you never know what interest you may spark. Perhaps a child will want to learn how to make their own ice cream on National Ice Cream Day or want to check out books from the library to understand the history of Groundhog Day. Regardless, these timeless activities are all planned out for you so that you can maximize your time with the student and reduce the administrative work of pulling plans together.

Regardless of how many of these ideas you choose to incorporate into your lesson plans and curriculum, this will be your go-to guide for all things fun and entertaining for your classroom. It can be modified based on age group.

Your students are sure to love it, and who knows, maybe you will learn a thing or two along the way!

I've also included a list of supplies that you might need for these activities so that you can ask your center or director to make sure they're available. If that's not an option for you, you can also create a "donation" drive each month to get parents to provide some of the supplies you'll need (they might even come in and volunteer to help on the days that they want to help you celebrate!)

While all of these activities are designed to help you reduce the amount of time spent on busy work and administrative tasks, I also know that not every day in the classroom goes the way you hoped it would, and sometimes the stress of a relationship with a colleague or a parent can really get you down (or make your blood boil!) I want to give you something that not only helps you engage your students, but also helps you manage your stress and anxiety, so I worked with illustrator Natalia Scabuso to create an adult coloring page for you to complete each month.

Spending time coloring is a little bit like meditation, and many clinical therapists assert that an hour spent quietly coloring can be as valuable as spending an hour meditating or exercising. It utilizes both sides of your brain and allows you to exercise your problem solving and organizational brainpower in a low risk, emotionally satisfying & creative activity.

Burnout is a huge risk for early childhood educators, so any time you're feeling a little frayed around the edges or falling a little out of love with the work you do, flip to your month, grab the crayon tub and allow yourself a little time to unwind and relax.

Childcare workers, early childhood educators, and teachers are incredible, and the work you do to build the foundation for childhood development has a direct impact on the world around us and the kind of society we will have in the future. I am so grateful to you for every book you read, every sticky finger and runny nose you wipe, every building block you clean up, and all of the hard work you put in behind the scenes to create an environment where our children can grow and thrive.

Don't ever forget that you are amazing, and you are appreciated every single day. One day, a child like me will grow up and remember everything you did to bring joy and celebration into her life!

JANUARY

JANUARY

January 1

Celebrate: New Year's Day

What You'll Do:
It's a brand-new year! What will it hold? Discuss the possibilities and traditions with the children. Perhaps have some traditional New Year's food (black-eyed peas, turnip greens). Enjoy the promise of a new year!

Infant/Toddler Adaptation:
Our youngest students can also participate by trying new foods and ringing in the New Year!

January 2

Celebration: Winter Animals

What You Will Need:
Books, pictures, figures

What You'll Do:
We know children are drawn to nature. Let's talk to them about animals who thrive in the winter. Snow leopards, reindeer, and snowshoe hares are just a few that come to mind. Explore their habitats and what part of the world they live in. Share their names and help children identify them. Allow the children to play with figures and recreate the habitats and things they've learned.

Infant/Toddler Adaptation:
Ensure that the figures are not choking hazards. Allow the children to explore. Name the animals, a few a time, in a clear distinct voice. Have the chilcren repeat.

January 3

Celebration: Straw Day

What You Will Need:

Various straws, size and colors, biodegradable straws

What You'll Do:

Who doesn't love a straw? Children are drawn to the colors, stripes, bendy and swirly straws. There are unlimited possibilities on how to incorporate them in the classroom. For lunch or snack time, provide bendy or swirly straws for some fun. Maybe even allow for some bubble blowing fun! If you want to introduce some environmental aspects, introduce paper straws and discuss why they are important to the environment.

Infant/Toddler Adaptation:

Use containers with various size openings for our youngest friends to insert straight straws into, the smaller the opening the more difficult, so increase the difficulty as you go. This will help with concentration and hand-eye coordination.

January 4

Celebration: Braille Day

What You Will Need:
The Braille Alphabet, Books written using Braille

What You'll Do:
Introducing children to Braille is an excellent way to incorporate empathy and understanding to the classroom. Young children are very tactile, so touching the pages will be sure to fascinate! You can learn to create words in Braille or perhaps their names. You can also incorporate stories about Helen Keller to bring a sense of familiarity to this project.

January 5

Celebration: Bird Day

What You Will Need:

Bird Charts, Field Guides, Binoculars, Bird feeders,
Books about birds

What You'll Do:

We all know young children are drawn to nature. We can help encourage this and foster their love of nature by providing them several opportunities to learn more. Try posting a chart or poster of local birds by a window. Children can quickly refer to it as they spot birds outdoors. Putting a bird feeder near that window will increase the opportunities children will have to see birds. Field guides will also help identify birds. Take one along on a nature walk or a quick trip to the park or playground. Children will love he opportunity to see birds up close using binoculars. Keep a pair near the window or bring them along with your field guide.
You can always read books about birds of the world, or specific regions. Use bird flash cards to introduce the names of birds not found locally. Trips to the Zoo or nature preserves could also be in order.

Infant/Toddler Adaptation

You can use charts and feeders, too. Name the birds for the children and have them repeat the names.

January 6

Celebration: 3 Kings Day, Apple Tree Day, Bean Day

What You Will Need:
Books, apples, beans

What You'll Do:
If you celebrate 3 Kings Day, often called Epiphany, there are so many fun things to do. Introducing the young child to the three wise men in a concrete way brings the Christmas story to life for our young charges. We know children identify with concrete objects, so a nativity they can manipulate would be ideal! Providing three small gifts, just would also be a lovely way to celebrate. Learning how Epiphany is celebrated around the world would also be interesting to our young friends.

Apple Tree Day is such an interesting day! Learning about (and sampling) the many different species of apples would be delightful.

Pair this with Bean Day and you will have a huge hit on your hands! There are so many kinds of beans, the possibilities are endless!
In a classroom setting, have the children bring a different kind of apple and bean each and create a small taste testing event. Yum!

Infant/Toddler Adaptation
Soft Nativities are an option. Name each person and have the children repeat the names. For apple or bean day, applesauce is always a hit. Soft beans are delicious and wonderful for our small friends!

January 7

Celebration: Rock Day

What You Will Need
Rocks

What You'll Do
Here's another themed day where the sky is the limit! Children love rocks, reintroduce the idea of a pet rock, create a rock garden in the classroom, or go for a nature walk or tour the playground and gather rocks. Come back and identify what the children have gathered. The art projects are also plentiful. Painting rocks is always hit with young children. Arranging smaller stones into collage would be a fun guided group project.

Infant/Toddler Adaptation
Collecting rocks, ensuring they are large enough not to be a choking hazard is a fun option. Sorting them by color or placing them in different containers is another.

January 8

Celebration: Bubble Bath Day

What You Will Need
Bubble supplies

What You'll Do
Bath time may not be possible at school but preparing for a bubble bath when the children get home could be fun. Perhaps making a small bit of bubble bath for later would be a fun project. If the weather is cold and outdoor time is sparse, movement is still necessary for our small friends. Pretending to take a bath could be fun using all kind of silly stretches or scenarios- (oh no, I think we used too much bubble bath! - Moving arms wildly to clear the imaginary bubbles). Hilarity is sure to ensue!

Infant/Toddler Adaptation
Blowing bubbles is an alternative the children are sure to love.

January 9

Celebration: Law Enforcement Appreciation Day, Static Electricity Day

What You Will Need
Thank you notes, a balloon

What You'll Do
We should always show appreciation for community workers and introducing this feeling of gratitude to our young friends is an important part of our work. Try writing thank you notes to your local law enforcement agencies. You could also invite them to speak with the children. Maybe baking treats to be delivered would be fun, or having the officers come share the treats with the children would be even better!

Static electricity is just one of the amazing wonders of childhood. The tried and true balloon trick is an absolute favorite. Explore different scenarios, and counteracting tricks such as dryer sheets or lotion. Explain what causes static electricity and why these counteracting tricks work. If you have a space that can be darken, enjoy watching the sparks fly!

Infant/Toddler Adaptation
If you would like to make cards, stamps and stickers are a great option for small hands. Small children can appreciate static electricity, too!

January 10

Celebration: Houseplant Appreciation Day

What You Will Need

houseplants, child-sized gardening tools, a watering can, a mister

What You'll Do

Small children have such a large capacity for love. We can foster their love of nature by showing them how to care for plants. Introduce a non-toxic indoor plant to the children. (Aloe plants are hardy and can withstand a lot of "love" or neglect.) Provide opportunities for the children to care for the plant. They can learn to dead-head, water, and use the mister to clean the leaves. Creating a watering chart or teaching the children to leave some sort of marker (a stone, small sign, etc.) in the plant will alert others that the plant has been watered. Children will enjoy learning about and meeting the needs of the plant. When we introduce these small lessons to our children, we help them to become good stewards of the earth.

Infant/Toddler

Adaptation Our youngest students should have non-toxic plants to care for as well. Take extra care in showing them how to water, perhaps only filling a watering can with a minimal amount of water.

January 11

Celebration: Learn Your Name in Morse Code Day, Splash in a Puddle Day

What You Will Need
Morse Code Chart, Puddles

What You'll Do
Young children are often just learning the alphabet and it's sounds. What a great way to spark new interest by introducing Morse Code. Help the children find the code for the letters in their names. Write secret message or play spy games with the children depending on their abilities and interest.

Splash in a puddle day, depending on what region you happen to live, puddle may not be available or the best idea in January. However, if the conditions are right, what could be more fun?

Infant/Toddler Adaptation
Our young friends may love puddles even more than our EC friends. Have a change of clothes ready and head outside!

January 12

Celebration: Pharmacist Day

What You Will Need:
Thank you notes

What You'll Do:
Showing gratitude for those who care for us is imperative. Modeling these sentiments is what we are called to do. Try writing thank you notes to your pharmacists. You could also invite them to speak with the children. Maybe baking treats to be delivered to the pharmacy would be possible or inviting the pharmacists to come speak and share with the children would be a huge hit for everyone!

Infant/Toddler Adaptation:
If you would like to make cards, stamps and stickers are a great option for small hands.

January 13

Celebration: Sticker Day, Rubber Ducky Day

What You Will Need:
Stickers, Rubber Duckies, small pool

What You'll Do:
We know how much young children love stickers! Provide papers for the children to create art projects using stickers. They could illustrate creations to go along with their stickers or create counting projects.

Rubber duckies are a childhood favorite. Bath time at school is not exactly feasible, but there are plenty of ways to play! Fill a small pool with water and float the duckies. Maybe have a race or play math games with the ducks. (How many yellow ducks crossed the line in the pool? Or write numbers on the ducks and add their sums). Sing the childhood classic, Rubber Ducky as you enjoy hours of Rubber Ducky fun!

Infant/Toddler Adaptation:
Young children can participate in these days, too! Adapt as you see fit for your class.

January 14

Celebration: International Kite Day

What You Will Need:

Kites, books about kites

What You'll Do:

We all have fond memories of kite flying, so let's pass that on to our children! Kites are so fun and there are so many types. Read about kites with the children. If weather permits, try to fly a kite. If that's not a possibility art projects creating kites is a great alternative.

Infant/Toddler Adaptation:

Provide a drawing of a kite for the children to color. Name it and name the colors as you go.

January 15

Celebration: Martin Luther King Jr's Birthday, Strawberry Ice Cream Day

What You Will Need:

Books about MLK, strawberry ice cream

What You'll Do:

Introduce MLK to young children through books or maybe a short video. Combine the themes by have some strawberry ice cream in honor of his birthday.

Infant/Toddler Adaptation:

Everyone loves strawberry ice cream, if diets won't allow for it for our youngest friends, adapt by mashing strawberries. Perhaps add a bit of yogurt and freeze or chill.

January 16

Celebration: Appreciate a Dragon Day

What You Will Need:
Books about dragons, photos, figures

What You'll Do:
There are so many things you could do today! Reading about mythical dragons in a variety of cultural settings will dazzle the children! Introducing a "real" dragon- the Kimodo Dragon is sure to be a huge h t. Children can create their own dragon stories, draw pictures, or play with dragon figures to help celebrate this super fun day!

January 17

Celebration: Kid Inventor's Day

What You Will Need:
a variety of odds and ends, book about inventors, simple machines- if available

What You'll Do:
Inventors have changed our world. There is no doubt that the children we work with each day are capable of being the next life-changing inventor. Let's foster their creativity and get them dreaming of amazing things! Read about several inventors, introduce the inventions or demonstrate simple machines. Have a small makers table where children can use their imaginations and create some brand new inventions! You never know what may spark the next big idea!

January 18

Celebration: Winnie the Pooh Day

What You Will Need:

Books by A. A. Milne

What You'll Do:

Most children will know who Winnie the Pooh is. Share a few passages from the beloved children's books. Discuss the wisdom and lessons gleaned by such a sweet old bear. Children could bring their own Winnie, wear Winnie clothes, or perhaps drawing their favorite scenes would be fun. What a great day!

January 19

Celebration: Popcorn Day, Tin Can Day

What You Will Need:
Popcorn- varieties of flavors, Tin Cans

What You'll Do:
Everyone loves popcorn. January is a month where the weather isn't always great so maybe plan a movie day and provide all kinds of flavors of popcorn. Plain old buttered or even natural are also a great go to!
For Tin Can Day, you can introduce all kinds of fun. Make tin can telephones and see if you can decipher what each other is saying. Play Kick the Can. Use the tin cans as planters and plant seeds to be transplanted in spring. See January 26th.

Infant/Toddler Adaptation:
Children can participate with the tin cans as you see fit. Popcorn may be a choking hazard.

January 20

Celebration: Cheese Lover's Day, Penguin Appreciation Day

What You Will Need:
Cheese, Penguin books, photos, figures

What You'll Do:
Provide different variety of cheeses for the children to sample. Discuss where they come from. Discuss how cheese is made.

Children just love penguins! Provide books and photos of penguins, introduce the different spec es of penguins and what regions of the world they are found. Allow the children to play with the figures, perhaps using them as models for art projects or penguin booklets.

January 21

Celebration: MLK Day (observed), Squirrel Appreciation Day, Granola Bar Day, Playdate Day, National Hug Day

What You Will Need:

Books on MLK, squirrel books, photos figures, Granola bars

What You'll Do:

Continue to discuss MLK and all of his wonderful contributions to our world. Squirrels are the best! Provide books and photos of squirrels, introduce the different species of squirrels and what regions of the world they are found. Allow the children to play with the figures. Introduce the song "Grey Squirrel".

Isn't every day Granola Bar Day in an early childhood environment. Celebrate this childhood staple by hosting a taste-test party and have the children vote for their favorite one.

Playdates are becoming more and more popular and our young friends are just beginning to experience this. Have a volunteer coordinate playdates for the class.
*Careful to ensure that no one is left out!

National Hug Day might be the best day ever. Share the love with the children! Let's also use this as a time to teach children about boundaries and asking to hug someone before touching them. Teaching children that they don't have to hug if they don't want to may seem like a downer on such a joyful day, but it's an important grace and courtesy lesson that can be invaluable to our young friends.

January 22

Celebration: Hibernation and Migration

What You Will Need:
Books, maps about migration

What You'll Do:
children love to learn about animals and their habitats. Introduce the concepts of hibernation and migration to the young child. Read stories, show maps showing migratory patterns of birds other species, and give examples of familiar animals and their hibernation or migratory patterns.

Name the animals and their habitats.

January 23

Celebration: Handwriting Day, Measure Your Feet Day

What You Will Need:

Lined paper, pencils, construction paper and rulers

What You'll Do:

Two super fun experiences. Children typically write before they read, so their interest in writing should be peaked. Make a handwriting station for the children to practice writing their names, favorite words and phrases, or even write a story.

Measuring your feet can be very interesting. Comparing your measurements with your friends, tracing your foot and measuring it in inches and centimeters, and discussing how the measurements translate in to shoe sizes are just a few ideas that would delight the young child.

Infant/Toddler Adaptation:

Children can participate with measuring their feet, perhaps turning it into a sweet keepsake for parents would be a special thing.

January 24

Celebration: Belly Laugh Day

What You Will Need:

joke books, silly photos

What You'll Do:

Gather the children and start the giggles. Belly laughing has so many benefits and it's contagious. Perhaps tell a few jokes or show a few silly photos, once the laughter begins, it won't be long before everyone is cracking up. Showing children that it's ok to laugh in the classroom and sharing joy are such important lessons for young children!

January 25

Celebration: Chinese New Year

What You Will Need:

Books, the Chinese Zodiac Calendar, Chinese food, Chinese objects

What You'll Do:

Read about Chinese New Year, explore the zodiac and share with the children what animal represents them. Sample authentic Chinese food discuss the ingredients and where they come from. If you have any objects, share them and discuss. The possibilities are endless! We should always make every effort to share these holidays in a respectful, authentic way. If possible have someone from China to come and celebrate with the children. We should always remember to avoid stereotypes or derogatory depictions and be mindful of what we are representing to the children.

Stamps and stickers would be fun.So would painting or coloring their Chinese zodiac animal.

January 26

Celebration: Seed Swap Day

What You Will Need:
Seeds!

What You'll Do:
We know there is nothing better than relating one thing to another, if you have your Tin Can planters from a week ago, you can use them to plant the seeds the children bring in to share. Ask each child to bring in a packet of seeds or seed pod to share. Plant them in your Tin Can planters or other seedling starters in preparation for spring gardens.

Infant/Toddler Adaptation:
Children can participate, one pack of seeds and perhaps one pot for the class or seed starters to take home would work for this group.

January 27

Celebration: National Geographic Day

What You Will Need:
National Geographic Magazines

What You'll Do:
National Geographic Magazines are absolute treasures in the early childhood classroom. We can introduce literally anything in our world to the children through the pages of the magazine. Gather old copies and have the children explore them. Discuss what they find. Maybe have them cut out photos and make collages or booklet about their favorite regions of the world. Create animal booklets, continent folders or use the maps and other inserts for all sorts of learning opportunities.
Glue sticks and pre-cut pictures would make it easier for the children to manage.

January 28

Celebration: Blueberry Pancake Day

What You Will Need:
Pancake batter, blueberries, butter, syrup, whip cream
and a griddle

What You'll Do:
Who wouldn't love a blueberry pancake breakfast,
snack or even lunch? Check the dietary guidelines and
then get to griddling! Have the children mix the batter,
mixing in blueberries as they go. Once you have enough,
help the children pour the mix onto the griddle, safety
first, so if this isn't feasible, do it for them, but try to include
them in all the other steps. Top with butter, syrup or whip
cream and more fresh blueberries. Enjoy!

Infant/Toddler Adaptation:
Children can participate as you see fit

January 29

Celebration: Puzzle Day

What You Will Need:

Puzzles

What You'll Do:

Puzzles are such fun and we must remember to allow children time to work on them. In our busy word, we often rush not allowing for time for things like puzzles. Puzzles help the young child to build concentration. Provide numerous puzzles of various levels and difficulties for the children to work on. Allow the children to trade and try other puzzles. Take photos of the finished puzzles with the children who completed them. Celebrate their accomplishments and encourage cooperation.

Use simpler age appropriate puzzles and increase the difficulty as the children master each puzzle.

January 30

Celebration: Hockey

What You Will Need:

Books, photos or short videos about hockey.
Various real items from the sport

What You'll Do:

introducing young children to new sports can be fun. Children may see hockey on TV at home or may have relatives that play. Reading books sharing photos or even short videos about hockey will help children understand the concept of this sport. Sharing real items such as a hockey puck or ice skates and introducing new terms like Zamboni can be very interesting and fun for the young child. If you have the space and child size hockey sticks you can let the children experiment with hitting pucks into a net or a specific area. If hockey is a feasible sport to introduce, consider other winter sports.

Infant/Toddler Adaptation:

Children can participate, maybe naming items like skate, puck, hockey, and Zamboni would work. Perhaps hockey flash cards or naming cards would work well for this group.

January 31

Celebration: Backwards Day

What You Will Need:
a mirror

What You'll Do:
Backwards Day might be the best day of the year for our young friends. Children are just learning about the order of the world around them, creating an "alternate backwards" atmosphere is not only appealing it's hilarious! Use a mirror to help the children write or draw backwards. Children can wear their clothes backwards. Maybe try to pronounce words backwards. Walk backwards throughout the day or sit facing in the opposite directions. Follow the children's lead as they will think of so many "backwards" opportunities. Encourage as many as you can safely. What an awesome day!

Infant/Toddler Adaptation:
Children can participate, but they are just learning to get things right. It may confuse them. Try walking backwards on a taped line on the floor. Provide a mat if you feel they may need it.

FEBRUARY

FEB

UARY

February 1

Celebration: Bubblegum Day, World Read Aloud Day

What You Will Need:
Bubblegum, Books

What You'll Do:
Bubblegum, bubblegum in a dish, how many activities do you wish? As much fun as Bubblegum Day could be, remember to be safe as it could be a choking hazard. For those children who can chew gum, blowing bubbles might be the best thing ever! Take some cute pictures of the children as their bubbles are just about to pop. Create a collage of all the photos. Discuss the history of gum, where it comes from, and how it's made.

World Read Aloud Day can be celebrated by inviting families or local guests to come read to the children. Perhaps find a short chapter book and have people come in throughout the day to read a chapter at a time until the completion of the book. (Ensure that the children are sitting for long amounts of time at any given sitting). By the end of the day, the children would have heard an entire book. How fun!

February 2

Celebration: Groundhog Day,
Ice Cream for Breakfast Day

What You Will Need:

Books and Photos about Groundhog Day, Ice Cream

What You'll Do:

Will the Groundhog see his shadow? And what does it mean if he does or doesn't? Read and explain to the children about Groundhog Day. Share photos or a short video of Punxsutawney Phil. You can always incorporate a few fun facts about groundhogs or Philadelphia in the lessons.

Is ice cream for breakfast a good idea for young children? Probably not, but if you could somehow incorporate it, wouldn't it be a bit magical? Try a fruit sorbet or natural banana ice cream recipe if the sugar overload first thing in the morning is worrisome. We must remember that even though we are charged with looking out for the children's best interest, sometimes a little whimsy is just right.

February 3

Celebration: Black History Activities

What You Will Need:
Books, photos, stories short videos.

What You'll Do:
Share the accomplishments of African American with young children. There are so many great stories to share consider a variety of backgrounds (music, art, science, sports, peacemakers, inventors, religious leaders etc.). For the young child hearing stories and seeing African Americans represented in positive ways in your classroom are imperative to forming concepts and ideas that they will carry with them throughout their lives. We should not just limit this exposure to the month of February, but rather shine an extra spotlight on what we are already doing and dive deeper into the stories and lessons.

February 4

Celebration: Thank a Letter Carrier Day, Homemade Soup Day

What You Will Need:

Thank you notes, a letter and envelope template, Stone Soup (book)

What You'll Do:

We should continue to carry on our appreciation for our community workers. Writing letters to our letter carriers would be a lovely gesture. Use a template for how to write a letter and how to address and envelope. Inviting the postal workers to the classroom is also an option, although time may be a factor for them.

The book Stone Soup is a childhood classic that children just adore. Having each child bring one ingredient for a delicious vegetable soup would be so sweet. Reading the book and creating a similar concoction would be an exciting implementation of a darling classroom lesson.

February 5

Celebration: Weatherman's Day, School Counseling Week

What You Will Need:
Thank you notes, weather charts

What You'll Do:
Meteorologists are incredibly valuable members of our community and we should show them how much we appreciate them. Reading about weather, inviting local meteorologist to the classroom, and sending treats or thank you notes would be such a kind gesture. Charting the weather each day is a staple in the early childhood classroom. Discussing this with our esteemed guest makes it so much more comprehendible. If your school has a school counselor, it's also a great idea to show them some appreciation and love.

February 6

Celebration: Music Appreciation Month

What You Will Need:
Various forms of music

What You'll Do
introduce the children to various forms of music by sharing audio or short video recordings. Peter and the Wolf and Carnival of the Animals are two excellent sources to help encourage the young child to develop a love and appreciation of music.

February 7

Celebration: Send a Card to a Friend Day

What You Will Need:
Cards, art supplies, home addresses

What You'll Do:
We can continue to help the children develop their love of writing and develop empathy and feelings for their friends. After speaking with your local letter carrier or discussing our postal system, children should be familiar with mail. Help the children create cards and letters to send their friends. Gather the children's home addresses and send the cards and letter through the mail. The children will feel so special when they receive their sweet messages!

February 8

Celebration: Opera Day, Kite Flying Day

What You Will Need:
Books about Opera and Kites, Opera Recordings

What You'll Do:
We should never underestimate the young child. Opera is a beautiful art form and young children can appreciate the beauty if we introduce them to it. There are so many performances to share, so we should find a few and share with the children. Reading stories about attending an opera may
help children relate.

Kites are always a hit. We can build on what we did from Jan. 14 or this may the first time we are introducing kites. Weather may play a part on how much you are able to do. If you are able to get outside, fly a kite! If not, more art projects may be in the works. Make the most of what you are able to do.

February 9

Celebration: Pizza Day

What You Will Need:

Pizza crust, tons of toppings, small pizza tins and a toaster oven

What You'll Do:

There are several ways to make small pizza's so adapt a way that works for your situation. The most important thing would arguably be the toppings! Introduce lots of veggies. Children may not have experience them on a pizza, but may find they like them on a pizza. If cooking just isn't possible, try a no-cook fruit pizza with a shortbread or other prepared crust and add all kinds of fruits and try a yogurt "sauce". Yum!

February 10

Celebration: Umbrella Day

What You Will Need:
Umbrellas, cloud activities, Precipitation/watercycle lessons

What You'll Do:
So, umbrellas are so fascinating to young children. There are so many ways to explore the use of umbrellas. Introducing young children to precipitation and water cycle lessons is one way. Studying the various forms and types of clouds is another. There are many art projects involving umbrellas that children can participate in as well. If today happens to be a rainy day, try to get out and make use of your umbrellas!

February 11

Celebration: Make a Friend Day

What You Will Need:
Books on new friends, friendships

What You'll Do:
Making new friends can be intimidating for adults, but the young child has a natural capacity to love. In order to foster this, we must encourage children to seek out new friendships. Typically, young children don't need our interference, so we must be careful not to squash this sweet nature. Telling a child to make a new friend or to seek out someone new isn't really necessary. Sharing stories about meeting new friends should plant the seed. Children will seek out new friends organically, we must encourage this in our classrooms by providing social situations and opportunities to play. Even parallel play should be encouraged and supported at this age.

February 12

Celebration: Music Appreciation Month

What You Will Need:

Books, photos and when possible, real example of instruments

What You'll Do:

Introduce the young child to various instruments by sharing books and photos and when possible real examples of instruments. You can invite local musicians to share their talents with the children. If possible a trip to a musical performance would be ideal. If this is not possible short videos of famous musical performances would be another way to introduce instruments to children.

February 13

Celebration: Get a Different Name Day

What You Will Need:
Name tags

What You'll Do:
Talk to the children about names, origins and meanings. Tell them that just for one day they could change their name to anything they want. Record their names on their tags and try to refer to them by their "different" name. Young children will enjoy this and may develop a new appreciation for their original name. We can join in the fun by choosing a different name, too

February 14

Celebration: Valentine's Day

What You Will Need:

Valentine party supplies, books about Valentine's Day, cupid, and other traditions. Card, envelopes etc

What You'll Do:

Most of us have Valentine's Day activities that we love to do each year. Incorporate a few lessons in the middle of all of the festivities. Remember to provide the children with some sort of bag or envelope to carry goodies home. Helping the children create a Valentine for their parents/guardians is a lovely and sometimes overlooked gesture. We can also create cards for the troops, people in nursing homes or homeless shelters. Spreading love comes in a variety of ways. We should help the children to see that each day.

February 15

Celebration: Gumdrop Day

What You Will Need
Gumdrops, toothpicks, art supplies

What You'll Do
Celebrating a day dedicated to candy may not be ideal for the day after Valentine's day, but we can make it fun and educational. We could build structures using toothpick and gumdrops. Or how about some mosaics using gumdrops. It could be a super creative day-goody, goody gumdrops!

February 16

Celebration: Whale Appreciation Day

What You Will Need
Books, picture figures

What You'll Do
This could be a whale of a day! We can introduce all kinds of fun facts about Earth's largest mammals. Use the books and photos to help children identify all of the different species of whales. Allow children to play with the figures. Art projects are endless, think about a class underwater project. Each child could draw a whale and it could be incorporated into the larger project.

February 17

Celebration: President's Day

What You Will Need
Books about the Presidents, charts, videos

What You'll Do
While politics can be a bit dicey, the office of the president has been an institution since the beginning of our country. There are many ways to introduce presidents in a diplomatic way. We must remember not to impose our personal beliefs onto our young students. So, discussing fun facts about presidents from the past, important historical events that may have occurred during a particular presidency or how a president is elected are all new to our students. Showing short video clips of important, historic speeches, discussing who was president when they were born, when their parents/grandparents were born or even what we may remember about different presidents can be a great introduction to this important office.

February 18

Celebration: Black History Month

What You Will Need:
Invite local leaders to speak and visit with the children

What You'll Do:
Black history month is a time to celebrate the accomplishments of African-Americans in our communities. Inviting local leaders to come and visit with the children and provide positive role models is an excellent way to accomplish this.

February 19

Celebration: International Tug-O-War Day

What You Will Need:
A rope, line

What You'll Do:
Introduce this game to the children. Divide teams in multiple ways, boys vs girls, counting evens/odds, adults vs children, whatever works in your situation. Play multiple games, and encourage good sportsmanship. Congratulate the winning team each round. Model this for the children. This can be a dangerous game, and has had a bit of controversy so be mindful of any dangers and remember safety is paramount.

February 20

Celebration: Library Lovers Month

What You Will Need:

Library Cards! Library field trips

What You'll Do:

Encourage parents to obtain library cards for the young children and their families. Encourage trips to the library and if possible arrange field trip so that children can experience what libraries are like. Share with children all of the possible things that can be accomplished in the library including storytimes , reading, checking out books, videos, computer use, research and many other amenities.

February 21

Celebration: Introduce a Girl to Engineering Day

What You Will Need:
Books about female engineers, engineering

What You'll Do:
while most of us have girls AND boys in our classes, we have to admit there is a shortage of women in engineering fields. How can we encourage our girls and still be mindful of our male students?

Introducing our entire class to stories about engineering and female engineers is just the way to do it. By showing our class that engineering is a field that anyone can excel in takes any stigma away and encourages any student to pursue that field. Your friends have a lot of time before they decide which direction their lives may go. But we can plant positive seeds that may help them later in life. We have such an awesome responsibility to our children, we must remember to be mindful and encourage our future engineers!

February 22

Celebration: World Yoga Day

What You Will Need:
Yoga Cards, Yoga Mats.

What You'll Do:
What a lovely addition to any early childhood classroom! If you do not happen to practice yoga or cannot teach the poses, a small deck of yoga cards or short video clips may be a good substitute. Provide a few mats and either demonstrate or use examples of how to do each pose. Children can choose which pose they would like to try and when they are finished, they could roll their mat and return it ready for the next person. Having short yoga classes by certified child yoga instructors is the ideal, but when that's not available, providing a new way for movement is excellent for young children.

February 23

Celebration: 100th Day of School

What You Will Need:
100 items

What You'll Do:
While the actual 100th day of school may vary here are some fun things that you can do to celebrate. Counting to 100, collecting 100 objects in various forms. Doing different activities (jumping, humming, etc) for 100 seconds. Providing 100 things for snacks for a 100 party.

February 24

Celebration: Music Appreciation Month

What You Will Need:

Examples of music from different parts of the world.

What You'll Do:

Introduce children to various examples of music from different parts of the world. Do you know what a didgeridoo sounds like, or what part of the world it comes from? What about a mbira or djembe? Learn about what they sound like, where they originated from and hear how they are used to make music along with the children. Incorporate few geography lessons as you go!

February 25

Celebration: Play Cards Day, Fat Tuesday

What You Will Need:

cards, Mardi Gras themed items, books and photos, King Cake

What You'll Do:

Cards are not always easy for young children to follow. Simple games like Go Fish and Old Maid may even be a bit hard for our young friends. Introducing the suits, counting with cards and even adding or subtracting may be an adaptable way to include everyone if you find some children are having difficulties.

Mardi Gras is such a fun time, but this day doesn't conjure up images of young children. We can find ways to introduce the facts and history of Mardi Gras to share with the children. King cakes are always a big hit, because everyone is looking for the hidden baby. If you are able, you can also have the children try a bit of Cajun food. Yum! Laissez les bon temps rouler!

February 26

Celebration: Tell a Fairytale Day, Ash Wednesday

What You Will Need:

Book of Fairytales, book picture about Ash Wednesday

What You'll Do:

Fairytales are familiar tales for a lot of children. For a growing number of children, they haven't been introduced. Fairytales have fallen out of fashion in recent years, for a variety of reasons. Choose a few to share with the children. Have some discussions. Encourage children to come up with alternate endings or fairytales of their own. Get creative and encourage the children to as well.

If you celebrate Ash Wednesday, read about the day, share photos and discuss what the children may experience. Even if you don't celebrate, it may be a good idea to discuss because children may encounter people who have received ashes.

February 27

Celebration: Pink Day, Polar Bear Day, Strawberry Day

What You Will Need:
Polar bear books, photos and figures

What You'll Do:
Pink day! What could be more fun? Have the children wear pink, paint pink picture and celebrate all things pink.

For polar bear day- read books and share photos of polar bears, the children can play with the figures. Discussing polar bears, their habitats and characteristics is sure to be a hit.

Who wouldn't want to celebrate strawberry day? What could be more delicious. Have the children sample strawberries. Plain, natural strawberries would be best as young children are learning to classify what they are tasting.

February 28

Celebration: Floral Design Day, Tooth Fairy Day

What You Will Need:

Flower arranging items- vases, funnels, doilies and flowers.
Books about the tooth fairy, different traditions when
children loose teeth from around the world

What You'll Do:

If you have a flower arranging area in your classroom,
this would be the perfect day to introduce some more
complex designs to the children. If not, introduce the art
of floral design to the children. Children are naturally
attracted to beauty and fresh flowers in the classroom is
a lovely way to incorporate that. Start by trimming the
flowers into shorter, more manageable stems, then show
children how to fil the vases with water using the funnel,
and arrange the stems in the small vases.
Have the children place these arrangements throughout
the classroom, placing doilies under each vase to
protect the furniture and define where the arrangement
should go.
If you discuss characters such as the Tooth Fairy, reading
books and sharing teeth stories is a great way to ease
anxiety about losing teeth. Reading books about
traditions surrounding children losing teeth is very
appealing to children. Throw your Tooth on the Roof, is a
great book to share!

February 29th

Celebration: Leap Year

What You Will Need:
Books, calendars

What You'll Do:
The concept of leap year can be a hard one to grasp for the young child. Reading about Leap year with the children can help. Sharing calendars is another way to illustrate this concept. Fun activities, like leaping like a lizard can be fun, but we must be careful to represent this concept in a clear and non-confusing way. We do not want the children to think the day has to do with jumping or reptile

MARCH

MA

CH

March 1

Celebration: Compliment Day, Pig Day

What You Will Need:
Books, picture and figures

What You'll Do:
We must always model grace and courtesy for our young children. Introducing the proper way to give a complement is an excellent way to do this. Gather a small group of children and deliver genuine compliments, encourage the children to practice modeling grace and courtesy as you have shown them. Read books and shares pictures about pigs allow the children to play with the figures discuss pigs roles in our daily lives. Children could do pig art projects, sing pig songs etc. Just don't pig out!

Infant/Toddler Adaptation:
Children can participate as you see fit, can't you just imagine those sweet pink piggie art projects. Or a pink footprint for their parents- showing them their piggies!

March 2

Celebration: Read Across America Day, Dr. Seuss Day

What You Will Need:
Books, Dr. Seuss themed items

What You'll Do:
Chances are you already celebrate Dr. Seuss Day in some capacity. Incorporate your celebration with read across America day. Visit www.nea.org for ideas that fit your classroom's plan. Popular ideas include dressing up as a Seuss character, reading Dr. Seuss books and recreating or coloring some of those iconic illustrations. Share about Dr. Seuss' life and work. This day is sure to be a favorite of the children, so go all out!

Infant/Toddler Adaptation:
Children can participate as you see fit

March 3

Celebration: World Wildlife Day, National Anthem Day

What You Will Need:
Books about wildlife, perhaps short videos or pictures, books about the National Anthem, a recording of the National Anthem

What You'll Do:
We can't say it enough children absolutely adore nature! Sharing books and videos or pictures about wildlife is always a favorite in the early childhood classroom.. Introducing artwork, studying habitats, or using figures to re-create what they've learned children are always happy studying about wildlife.

Many young children have not yet been exposed to our national anthem. Sharing a recording of the national anthem and reading books about its origin are great ways to introduce them to you this famous song. If you happen to sing the national anthem in your classroom or children are familiar with the national anthem, you can also share national anthems from other countries and introduce those to your students as well.

Infant/Toddler Adaptation
Children can participate as you see fit

March 4

Celebration: Fun Facts about Names Day

What You Will Need:
Baby Name Books

What You'll Do:
Children are very interested in the origin and meaning of their names. Looking up the definition or meaning of their names (or discussing with their parents beforehand) are fascinating to the young child. Create small definition cards for each child with what you were able to uncover about each of their names for the children to take home a share and discuss with their families.

Infant/Toddler Adaptation:
Children can participate as you see fit, although just talking about first, middle and last names would probably work best.

March 5

Celebration: Unique Names Day

What You Will Need:
see March 4

What You'll Do:
as you continue to explore the meaning of names, you may find that some of your students have non-traditional names. Today is their day to shine! Share stories about their names and how they came to be. A child's name is their very identity, so celebrating it's origin and in this case uniqueness is so valuable.

You could combine March 4 & 5 activities…
Infant/Toddler Adaptation: Children can participate as you see fit, perhaps talking about the adult or other children's names would be more relatable.

March 6

Celebration: Dentist Appreciation Day

What You Will Need:

Thank you notes, book or photos about dentists, possible treats

What You'll Do:

We continue to show our appreciation for people in our community that help us stay healthy and that includes our dentist. Encourage the children to help create thank you notes or invite local dentists to come to the classroom and share stories of what they do. If that's not possible using books or photos to help the children understand what would happen at a cental visit would be appropriate. Making treats to send to dentists is also another option.

Encourage good dental habits and if possible share toothbrushes, toothpaste or dental floss with your students.

Infant/Toddler Adaptation:

If you would like to make cards, stamps and stickers are a great option for small hands.

March 7

Celebration: National Craft Month

What You Will Need:

Various crafty items, place to store them
(a maker's table)

What You'll Do:

March is National Craft Month. Provide children with craft
items for *open-ended* creating. Rotate different items
throughout the month. You could provide a "gallery"
space where the children could display finished projects.
We must support the children's creative processes and
try to allow them to create on their own. Sometimes, we
may need to gently guide them away from thing like
over using the glue, or using all the feathers provided,
without squashing their creative process.

March 8

Celebration: National Women's Month

What You Will Need:
books, photos maybe short videos of prominent
and successful women from all walks of life
(music, arts, science, politics, inventors etc).

What You'll Do:
Throughout the month of March provide books and
photos of women, historical and current, that have
made significant impacts in history. For the young child
hearing stories and seeing women represented in positive
ways in your classroom are imperative to forming
concepts and ideas that they will carry with them
throughout their lives.

Infant/Toddler Adaptation:
Children can participate as you see fit,
subtly would be best.

March 9

Celebration: Music in our Schools Month

What You Will Need:
various musical instruments

What You'll Do:
Music plays such a big part in the early childhood classroom. Provide several musical instruments for children to explore and create musical sounds. You could model tempo, rhythm, and even tones for children to repeat and re-create.

Infant/Toddler Adaptation:
Children can participate as you see fit

March 10

Celebration: Pack Your Lunch Day

What You Will Need:
Parents to help children pack a lunch

What You'll Do:
You may be at a school where children pack a lunch every day, if that's the case encourage parents to allow children to choose what goes in their lunch on this particular day. If packing a lunch isn't a typical option this will be an exciting day where children could explore all kinds of lunch options from home. Either way, encourage healthy choices and new and interesting foods!

March 11

Celebration: Napping Day

What You Will Need:
Nap mats, blankets, pajamas

What You'll Do:
This day is sure to be a favorite of all early childhood educators. Today we could encourage good sleeping habits for our children. Children could come dressed in pajamas, bringing nap items even if they no longer a nap. We could read bedtime stories, go over bedtime routines, and discuss sleeping arrangements from different traditions around the world. All children could take a "great nap" while listening to relaxing music or bedtime story, encouraging them to relax their bodies and obtain a restful sleep.

Infant/Toddler Adaptation:
Children can participate as you see fit

March 12

Celebration: Plant a Flower Day

What You Will Need:
Seeds or flowering plants

What You'll Do:
Depending on your set up and the weather in your area, you can encourage children to either plant seeds or plant flowers in your schools garden. If the weather is still too cold, seeds would work best. If you still have any tin cans from Jan 19th, you could use them as planters. Children love to be a part of community projects, so planting flowers in a school garden is such a fitting activity.

March 13

Celebration: Jewel Day

What You Will Need:
a birthstone chart, a list of the children's birthdays, possible example of each stone

What You'll Do:
Children love learning about their birthdays and things that go along with them. They also love jewels, rocks, gemstones and other lovely natural stones. So what could be better than introducing the children to their birthstone? Using a list of the children's birthdays identify for each child what their birthstone is. Children will be enamored with their stones. If possible, provide examples of each stone in the classroom for children to touch and observe.

Infant/Toddler Adaptation:
Children can participate as you see fit, stones could be a choking hazard so individual cards, stones in clear boxes, or a chart may work better.

March 14

Celebration: Learn About Butterflies Day

What You Will Need:

Books about butterflies, photos and figures.
Also possible caterpillar hatching kits

What You'll Do:

Share with the children books and photos of various species of butterflies. Discuss where they live and allow the children to play with the figures. If possible have a caterpillar hatching kit so that the children can observe caterpillars hatching in the classroom and eventually you can release a beautiful butterfly. We must foster the child's love of nature and this is a lovely way to do so.

Charts and cards may be a way to adapt.

March 15

Celebration: National Craft Month cont.

What You Will Need:
several craft project with specific steps

What You'll Do:
Survey your craft supplies and finds 2 to 3 projects with specific steps for children to follow in order to complete a craft. While open ended crafting is fun and allows children to be creative, following steps that lead to a specific ending are also important in early childhood activities. Giving the children opportunities for both creative processes are important and help in their development.

March 16

Celebration: Corndog Day, Panda Day

What You Will Need:

Corndogs, Book, picture, and figures of pandas, bamboo

What You'll Do:

Corndog day is a winner in any young child's book! Enjoy this culinary delight with the children exploring different dipping sauces if possible.

Children are naturally drawn to pandas, Share books, pictures and allow children to play with figures. Children can also learn about the habitat of the panda and learn about bamboo. If you are able to obtain live examples of bamboo share with the children and allow them to observe and explore it. Children can create art projects of pandas or art projects using bamboo. The possibilities are infinite. Follow the children's lead and enjoy where it takes you!

Infant/Toddler Adaptation:

Children can participate as you see fit, cut the corndogs up for the children.

March 17

Celebration: St. Patrick's Day

What You Will Need:

Green outfits, Books, pictures or objects

What You'll Do:

Many of us have some sort of Saint Patrick's day ideas or plans for our classrooms. Share books pictures are objects relating to St. Patrick's Day with the children. Encourage the children to come to class dressed in green. Share St. Patrick's folklore and explain where the origins of some of those tales come from. We must also remember to be mindful when explaining holidays and traditions, we must be respectful and not to use any derogatory descriptions or stereotypes when explaining these to the children.

Coloring shamrock may be an easy way to participate.

March 18

Celebration: National Women's Month cont.

What You Will Need:
several guests

What You'll Do:
Invite several women perhaps local community leaders or successful business women, or doctors etc. to come and speak to the children and visit with your classroom. By providing children with real world examples of successful women in all walks of life, we are demonstrating in tangible ways that women can attain any goals. This is just as important for our boys to see as it is for our girls.

Infant/Toddler Adaptation:
Children can participate as you see fit, stories and photos would be a subtle way to introduce the children without confusing them.

March 19

Celebration: Music in our School's Month

What You Will Need:
instruments, enough for each child to have one

What You'll Do:
Host a concert in your classroom! March is Music in our Schools Month and what better way to celebrate than create joyful noises as a class? Invite other classes, parents or grandparents to hear these sweet melodies!

March 20

Celebration: World Storytelling Day

What You Will Need:
A local storyteller, if possible.

What You'll Do:
There is a true art form to storytelling. If possible invite a local storyteller to share their craft with your class. If you are unable to do so, there are still plenty of things that you can do to celebrate World Storytelling Day. You can tell stories with the children, encouraging them to add to a group story or tell short stories of their own. Discuss the parts of a good story; beginning, middle, and end, perhaps even sharing larger concepts like plot and characters. Record the stories either by video or jotting them down and build bigger projects like illustrating or acting them out. These activities can lead to so many different projects, follow your children and enjoy watching them create!

March 21

Celebration: Memory Day

What You Will Need:
not a thing

What You'll Do:
Memory can be a difficult concept for children to grasp. Children are still learning the concept of time. Discuss memories and explain the concept to the children. Encourage the children to share memories with you and the class. Be prepared for some funny memories! Share some of your memories from your childhood to help the children relate. This will be sure to be a memorable day!

March 22

Celebration: Windy Days

What You Will Need:
Books, photos, short video clips, bubbles, pinwheels, windsocks or windchimes

What You'll Do:
Read stories about wind you can include photos or short videos to show the power of the wind, wind energy (turbines or sailboats) and how people rely on wind. There are a variety of activities you do easily with the children. Go outside and ask the children to hold out their hands and feel the wind. Provide bubbles and pinwheels to watch the wind create movement. They can use their breath to blow a bubble or if it's windy enough you may be able to create a few through wind power! Hanging a windsock or windchime near a window will provide children the opportunity to observe and hear the wind's power.

Infant/Toddler Adaptation:
Children can participate as you see fit

March 23

Celebration: Chip and Dip Day

What You Will Need:
Various chips and dips

What You'll Do:
Another yummy day in the classroom! Provide the children with various chips and dips to sample. Encourage tasting different combinations and exploring new foods. You can expand these activities by discussing regions of the world where foods come from. You just can't beat chips and dip day!

Infant/Toddler Adaptation:
Children can participate as you see fit, perhaps with crackers or a more soluble alternative.

March 24

Celebration: Chocolate Covered Raisins Day

What You Will Need:

Chocolate covered raisins

What You'll Do:

Chocolate covered raisins are a preschool favorite! Provide the children with various chocolate covered raisins, perhaps white chocolate, dark chocolate, and milk chocolate. Allow them to taste them and compare the differences. Encourage as much descriptive language as possible. What a delicious way to encourage new adjective use. You can also incorporate taste sensations in these lessons (sweet, sour, salty, bitter). Who knew there was so much to a little chocolate covered raisin?

Infant/Toddler Adaptation

Children can participate as you see fit, remembering that this could be a choking hazard for some.

March 25

Celebration: Waffle Day

What You Will Need:

Waffle/Pancake mix, waffle maker, fruit toppings, whipped cream

What You'll Do:

here is another delicious day! Encourage the children to participate as much as possible in your classroom. Children can mix the batter, pour into the waffle maker, apply fruit toppings and whip cream, if applicable. Waffles are delicious and you can discuss their origin and history while you're preparing them. If cooking is not an option in your classroom, you could choose already prepared waffles and incorporate those into your lesson. When we cook with the children we should always model hygienic practices and when we eat with the children we should always model appropriate eating habits. Children are always looking to us to set a good example. Waffles make delightful learning tools!

March 26

Celebration: Purple Day

What You Will Need:
Purple clothes, purple items

What You'll Do:
It's time to celebrate all things purple! Have the children come into school wearing purple clothing. Eating purple foods, painting with purple paint, and exploring different shades of purple in the classroom are all fun ways to celebrate purple day. This is another day where possibilities are endless. Consider what you have available in your classroom and utilize the purpleness of it all!

March 27

Celebration: Manatee Appreciation Day, World Theatre Day

What You Will Need:
Books pictures and figures of manatees,
a possible field trip to a local theater

What You'll Do:
Read and share pictures and stories of manatees with the children. Encourage them to learn more about their habitats and regions where they are found. Allow the children to play with figures of manatees and re-create what they've learned.

Encourage open ended art projects.
If possible plan a field trip to a local theater to allow the children to experience a short play. If this is not a possibility perhaps you could invite a local theater troupe to your classroom. If this is not a possibility either, share a short play with the children and explain the concept of theater to them.

A short video or even an audio tape would be worth sharing with the children. Helping children develop a love of theater and all of the various art forms that go into creating a theater production is something that starts early and something that we must foster.

March 28

Celebration: Weed Appreciation Day

What You Will Need:
Books, picture or live examples

What You'll Do:
Introduce the concept of weeds to children explain their benefits and in some cases medicinal properties. Allow children to explore pictures or if possible live examples of plants that are considered weeds. A great book is Weeds Find a Way. Children can illustrate their favorite weed or possibly even taste a few weeds. We must remember to explain how to be safe when choosing what we put in our mouths, especially when dealing with young children.

In this case, tasting weeds may be confusing, try looking for dandelions and blowing the seeds instead.

March 29

Celebration: Piano Day

What You Will Need:

Books, picture or audio recordings of piano
performances

What You'll Do:

If you are lucky enough to have access to a piano,
please allow the children to hear various songs played
on it. Let them explore the keys and the sounds that they
make. If this is not possible allow the children to hear
audio recordings of various piano performances. Read
stories and share photos of pianos to allow children to
understand the history of the piano and ts importance in
creating some of our most treasures songs. You could
also play various songs and see if the children could pick
out the piano sounds in each song. You could also use
this as an introduction to orchestra ard the various
instruments of the orchestra.

March 30

Celebration: Walk in the Park Day, Pencil Day, Doctor's Day

What You Will Need:

Permission to go to the park, Pencils, Thank you notes or treats

What You'll Do:

Is there anything more relaxing than a stroll through the park? There are so many things that the young child can explore in our local parks. If you have access to the park obtain permission and allow your children a springtime stroll through the park. If this is not possible try to re-create a stroll on your playground or school grounds and if this is still not possible perhaps singing songs or reading stories about cars would be another option.

Pencil day sounds so fun. Allow children to use colored pencils or writing pencils in various ways to celebrate writing or drawing in the classroom. Share with children the history of writing and various writing utensils.

Again we show our appreciation for those who keep us healthy and strong by creating thank you's or making treats for our doctors. You can invite local pediatricians or other doctors to the classroom have discussions on healthy choices, our bodies or different types of doctors.

Infant/Toddler Adaptation:
If you would like to make cards, stamps and stickers are a great option for small hands.

March 31

Celebration: Crayola Crayon Day, Neighbor Day

What You Will Need:
Crayons

What You'll Do:
You can use Crayola Crayons to create beautiful picture to give to your neighbors! If the school has neighbors, this may be an option, you could consider a neighboring classroom neighbors, or encourage children to share with neighbors at home. We must remember to stress safety to the children unfortunately, the home option may not be wise. You can also check out fun ideas on the Crayola Crayon website.

Infant/Toddler Adaptation:
If you would like to make cards, stamps and stickers are a great option for small hands.

APRIL

APRIL

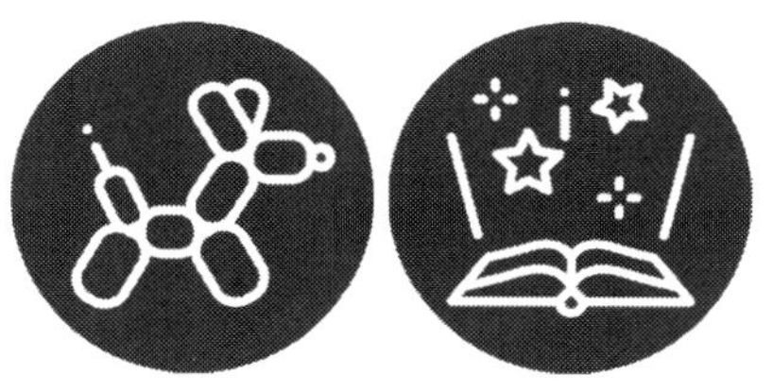

April 1

Celebration: April Fool's Day, Fun Day, Reading is Funny

What You Will Need:

Assortment of humorous or joke books

What You'll Do:

Celebrating April Fool's Day is hilarious. Young children love practical jokes. There are plenty of fun things you can incorporate throughout the day, that would fool everyone. We must remember to avoid anything that could be considered cruel, scary, or anything that could cause harm. The best prank we've seen for small children is- asking who wants brownies- of course everyone is excited- "Me! Me!", the children answer, the teacher then opens a pan and passes out the letter "e" cut out of brown construction paper. Get it? Brown "e's"? The children will giggle and definitely be disappointed, so make sure there are actual brownies on hand for a good laugh and a treat!

Reading limericks, jokes or funny stories goes along nicely with April Fool's Day and you can celebrate Reading is Funny Day, too!

Infant/Toddler Adaptation:
Children can participate as you see fit, perhaps avoiding any jokes today, they make not "get" them.

April 2

Celebration: Children's Book Day, PB & J Day, World Autism Day

What You Will Need:
Books, Peanut Butter and Jelly, Autism info

What You'll Do:
Read some of the favorites of the classroom or visit the library to pick a few new ones.

If you can have peanuts in your classroom, celebrate PB & J Day. Such a yummy childhood favorite! If there are allergies, substitute for a safer alternative where applicable.

Raising autism awareness is a huge part of our responsibilities as early childhood educators. You may have children with autism in your classroom, you may be searching for appropriate ways to bridge this topic with parents. Today, you can provide literature to you parents on appropriate behaviors and responses, or checklists on what to look for, or local agencies that can help families as they learn more about autism. Remember, we are often there during the initial diagnosis and parents need us and our support. Use this day to help fit these needs.

April 3

Celebration: World Party Day, Day of Hope, Find a Rainbow Day

What You Will Need:

Party supplies, slips of paper, prisms, flashlights

What You'll Do:

If the mood strikes you- throw a party! It may seem like there is a party for every occasion in the early childhood classroom. For this day, perhaps let the children plan and set up all of it. There is no "pressure" to get a bunch of holiday activities completed. So, the children can plan and execute a party on their own terms.

To celebrate Day of Hope, talk to the children about what hope means. Discuss their hope and dreams. Record them on pretty slips of paper with the dates.

Parents will appreciate these and they make wonderful keepsakes. Who knows- a child in you classroom may aspire to be president and 40 years from now may be in the White House!

Find a Rainbow Day is pretty dependent on weather conditions. If they don't happen to be conducive to rainbow producing, create your own using prisms! If it's an especially cloudy day, use flashlights to create rainbows all over the room.

April 4

Celebration: World Rat Day, Carrot Day

What You Will Need:
Books about rats, photos and figures, carrots

What You'll Do:
Read to the children about rats, their habitats and the interesting facts about them. Share photos and allow the children to play and explore the figures. If you have a rat as a class pet, perhaps plan some special activities around your class friend. 2020 is the Chinese new year of the rat, so you could also incorporate this in your daily activities.

Carrot day! Provide a variety of carrots- baby, stem on, colored, etc. and allow the children to sample and compare them. You could also provide a variety of dips or ask a volunteer to prepare a more complicated carrot dish (ex: carrot souffle) for the children to sample.

April 5

Celebration: Caramel Day, Read a Road Map Day

What You Will Need:

ingredients for homemade caramel (granulated sugar, kosher salt, water, heavy whipping cream, butter) hot plate, sauce pan, container. Road maps

What You'll Do:

Prepare caramel according to the recipe, allowing the children to participate as much as possible. If cooking is not an option, prepare the caramel ahead of time. Allow the children to sample the caramel and reserve some for tomorrow.

Provide a variety of road maps with different symbols on the keys. Explain what the symbols mean and explore the maps. Give simple directions for the children to follow. Allow the children to draw maps of their own. With the rise of GPS use in our society, scientist are saying that the navigation part of brains are slowly shrinking. This is a necessary skill, so even though it may seem obsolete, it's important! Have fun and get creative!

Sampling caramel and naming the map would be the first step in adaptation.

April 6

Celebration: Caramel Popcorn Day

What You Will Need:
Caramel from yesterday, popcorn

What You'll Do:
If you can, have a popcorn popper. How fun! If not, have the children combine the melted caramel and popcorn to make a yummy treat! Remember- hot caramel can burn, so use caution when allowing the children to help.

Infant/Toddler Adaptation:
Popcorn can be a choking hazard, proceed with caution.

April 7

Celebration: Beaver Day, World Health Day

What You Will Need:
Books about beavers, photos and figures, info and props about health

What You'll Do:
Read to the children about beavers, their habitats and the interesting facts about them. Share photos and allow the children to play and explore the figures.

You have probably celebrated a few health related days with the children by now, gather any info, props, literature, books etc and go over how to keep your students bodies healthy. Topics could include dental health, healthy eating habits, exercise, or good sleep habits. You can also talk about mental health, handwashing, ways to catch a sneeze or toileting habits. Consider issues that may be affecting your classroom or items you may have and focus on them. Children can always use gentle reminders and more info on how to stay healthy.

April 8

Celebration: Draw a Picture of a Bird Day, Zoo Lovers Day

What You Will Need:
Zoo field trip, paper and art supplies

What You'll Do:
Head to the Zoo! Make sure to visit the aviaries. Draw and sketch pictures of birds. If a field trip isn't possible, look out your window or consult the bird charts and books you may have in your room.

Infant/Toddler Adaptation:
Children can participate as you see fit, provide a drawn bird and allow them to color it.

April 9

Celebration: Name Yourself Day, Unicorn Day

What You Will Need:

See Feb 13, name tags, Unicorn books, photos figures

What You'll Do:

If you didn't get to celebrate then try it now. Talk to the children about names, origins and meanings. Tell them that just for one day they could change their name to anything they want. Record their names on their tags and try to refer to them by their "different" name. Young children will enjoy this and may develop a new appreciation for their original name. Wcan join in the fun by choosing a different name, too.

If you choose to celebrate Unicorn Day, remind the children that they are fantasy characters. Children are trying to order their world, so it's important to mention it. You can keep the day magical by sharing pictures, creating art projects or creating stories about unicorns.

April 10

Celebration: Sibling Day, International Safety Pin Day

What You Will Need:
Card making material, photos of siblings, Safety Pin Frames

What You'll Do:
Siblings are built in best buddies and we should encourage our students to have healthy relationships with their siblings. Discuss what siblings are, great ways to get along and how to be a good big/little sister/brother. Help the children create cards or pictures using photos sent in from families. If photos aren't available, have the children draw pictures of themselves and their siblings. If you have dressing frames/practice in your classroom, pull-out the safety pins and demonstrate how to use them. Some of the children may not be ready for this lesson, so use your best judgement.
Infant/Toddler Adaptation: Children can participate as you see fit, skip Safety Pin activities.

April 11

Celebration: Pet Day, Cheese Fondue

What You Will Need:

Photos of pets, art supplies, cheese fondue set and dipping foods

What You'll Do:

Pets are often a huge part of our students lives. Have the children draw pictures or use photos of their pets to create art projects. Talk about the importance of pets, how to care for pets, or the names of the children's pets and how they came to be. You could create a collage or scene using all of the pets of your classroom.

If you can come across a cheese fondue set, prepare the cheese and have the children dip different foods exploring the different combinations.

April 12

Celebration: Grilled Cheese Sandwich Day, Teach Your Children to Save Day

What You Will Need:
cheese, bread, butter, a griddle. Three jars

What You'll Do:
Have the children assist you in preparing grilled cheese sandwiches. You can use a variety of cheeses or add different toppings like bacon or tomato or ham to make the sandwiches extra yummy!

Prepare three jars on the first jar write "spend", second jar "give", and on the third jar "save". Discuss with the children how important saving and giving are when they come across money, just as important as spending. You can encourage the children to create their own jars at home or think of projects that you would like to spend money on, save some money for, and give money to for your class as a group. These early money lesson make a big impression on the children. Instilling these concepts early will help them later when allowances and holiday/birthday money come into play in a more real way.

Infant/Toddler Adaptation

Children can participate as you see fit, our young friends may not know what saving is, but introducing a piggy bank may help.

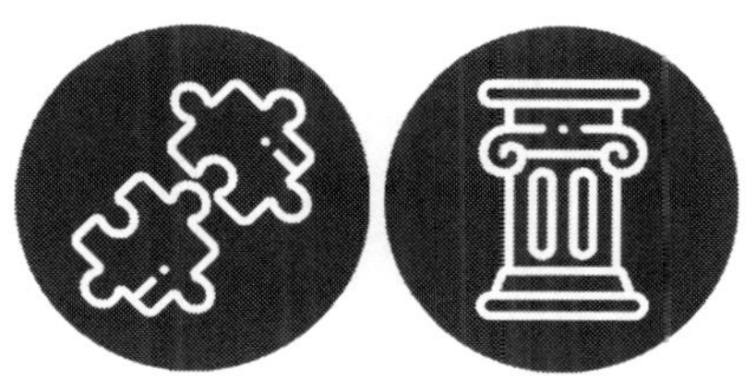

April 13

Celebration: Scrabble Day,
Thomas Jefferson Day

What You Will Need:
Old Scrabble tiles, Books about Thomas Jefferson, photos, copy of the Declaration of Independence

What You'll Do:
Read to the children about Thomas Jefferson, our third president. Share photos and allow the children to explore the Declaration of Independence.
Use old Scrabble tiles to form words. Our children are learning to read, form words or their names. What a fun way to encourage all of this. Play sound games or gather a few tiles and give their name and sound to children who are not yet reading.

Infant/Toddler Adaptation:
Children can participate as you see fit, perhaps providing them with the letters that make up their name and have them glue them would be fun.

April 14

Celebration: Look up at the Sky Day, Dolphin Day

What You Will Need:

Books about dolphins, photos and figures

What You'll Do:

Read to the children about dolphins, their habitats and the interesting facts about them. Share photos and allow the children to play and explore the figures.

Go outside, have the children look up at the sky. Enjoy! If you happen to have a cloudy day, look for shapes or figures in the clouds. Take some time to just appreciate the vast beautiful sky!

April 15

Celebration: ASL Day

What You Will Need:
American Sign Language chart or book

What You'll Do:
We keep saying it- children love language at this stage in their life. They soak it up! Incorporate some signs today to help introduce them to ASL. Some children may already have signs, encourage them to share. You can also help them sign their name. Or perhaps look up words for them and share. If you have access to a certified ASL instructor, invite them to your class to "talk" with the children.

Infant/Toddler Adaptation:
Children can participate as you see fit, our young friends may know signs for "thank you", "sleepy", or "hungry". If not, these would be great ones to introduce.

April 16

Celebration: Save the Elephants Day

What You Will Need:
Books about elephants, photos and figures

What You'll Do:
Read to the children about elephants, their habitats and the interesting facts about them. You can incorporate conservation topics, too. Share photos and allow the children to play and explore the figures.

April 17

Celebration: Bat Appreciation Day, Haiku Poetry Day

What You Will Need:

Books about bats, photos and figures, examples or books with Haiku poems

What You'll Do:

Read to the children about bats, their habitats and the interesting facts about them. Share photos and allow the children to play and explore the figures.

Share Haiku poems with the children. Talk about syllables and perhaps try to create a few Haiku poems of your own as a group. Don't worry if it seems a bit much for some children, do as much as your group can do. Planting the seeds for a love of poetry is just as great as the day the child fully understands!

April 18

Celebration: World Heritage Day

What You Will Need:
Books about cultural sites, photos and figures

What You'll Do:
Read to the children about cultural sites, their importance throughout history and the interesting facts about them. Share photos and allow the children to play and explore the figures. You can also pull out the globe or atlas to discuss where in the world each of these sites are located.

Infant/Toddler Adaptation
Children can participate as you see fit, name the sites and have the children repeat the names.

April 19

Celebration: Bicycle Day, Poetry & Creative Mind Day

What You Will Need:
children's bikes, helmets, safety pads, an empty parking lot or safe place to ride, poetry examples or books

What You'll Do:
Host a bike rodeo! Have the children bring in their bikes, trikes or other riding apparatus. Talk about bike safety, helmets, and knee and elbow pads. Have volunteers come to help or provide refreshments.

Read different types of poems to the children. See if they can hear the difference in the rhythm or rhyme.

Infant/Toddler Adaptation:
Children can participate as you see fit, or providing one riding apparatus for the classroom could be more manageable.

April 20

Celebration: Chinese Language Day, Volunteer Recognition Day

What You Will Need

Thank you cards, treats, Books or examples of Chinese writing.

What You'll Do

As we continue to model how to be appreciative, we must show the children how much we appreciate our volunteers. Have the children create cards or letters expressing your thanks for all of the wonderful deeds throughout the year. (A helpful hint, each day you have a volunteer in your room record it on your calendar, at the end of the year – today- it will be easy to remember who to thank.) The children can also make treats for the volunteers, look to see what you have on hand or what would be easy to create/make.

If you have a native Chinese speaker in your circle, invite them to share some writing samples with the class. If not books or other examples will work. Share with the children the examples, discuss the differences and ask the children to try to recreate a few words.

If you would like to make cards, stamps and stickers are a great option for small hands.

April 21

Celebration: World Creativity and Innovation Day, Kindergarten Day

What You Will Need:

a variety of odds and ends, book about inventors and innovators

What You'll Do:

Innovation has changed our world. There is no doubt that the children we work with each day are capable of being the next life-changing innovator. Let's foster their creativity and get them dreaming of amazing things! Read about several inventors and innovators. Have a small makers table where children can use their imaginations and create some brand new inventions!

You never know what may spark the next big idea! If you are a Kindergarten teacher- throw a party! If you have children headed to Kindergarten, make a visit to that classroom to help the children see what's in store. Skip the Kindergarten visit for now, their time is coming soon enough!

April 22

Celebration: Earth Day, Jelly Bean Day

What You Will Need:
Earth Day books, books about conservation or recycling, Jelly Beans

What You'll Do:
Read the books to the children. Discuss what you are currently doing in your classroom and what you would like to do in the future to help our earth. Celebrate all the wonderful things about our earth. Sometimes the state of the earth can be a heavy subject for adults, so imagine hearing it as child! Try to keep it light, but factual.
Jelly Bean Day could be so fun! Have a tasting party or contest, blindfold the children and see if they can guess what each flavor is. Try to avoid the "gross" jelly beans. Those can be saved for home!

Infant/Toddler Adaptation:
Children can participate as you see fit, jelly beans could be a choking hazard.

April 23

Celebration: World Book Night

What You Will Need:
Books, goodnight take home bags

What You'll Do:
Have the children choose one book to "check out' whether it be from the classroom or the library. Place them in a bag decorated with "sleepy" decorations. Have them take the books and bags home for a bedtime story. You can also include a note from you wishing them sweet dreams.

April 24

Celebration: Pig in a Blanket Day

What You Will Need:

Pigs in a blanket, premade or ingredients

What You'll Do:

Have the children help you prepare pigs in a blanket either in oven or premade. Discuss how this fun food got its name.

Infant/Toddler Adaptation:

Children can participate as you see fit, cut up the pigs for the children.

April 25

Celebration: World Penguin Day

What You Will Need:
Books about penguins, photos and figures

What You'll Do:
Read to the children about penguins, their habitats and the interesting facts about them. Share photos and allow the children to play and explore the figures.

Infant/Toddler Adaptation:
Children can participate as you see fit

April 26

Celebration: Pretzel Day, Alien Day

What You Will Need:
Pretzels, hard and soft, aliens

What You'll Do:
Provide the children with hard and soft pretzels. Allow them to taste them and sample the difference.
If you choose to participate in Alien Day there are a variety of things that you could do. Provide the children with different representations of aliens. Discuss aliens as much as you feel comfortable. Remember children are forming ideas about the world, so tread carefully. Perhaps you could skip the alien portion of the day.

April 27

Celebration: Tell a Story Day, Marine Mammal Day

What You Will Need:
Story paper, Marine animal books, photos and figures

What You'll Do:
Provide story paper for the children to draw a picture on. If they can, have them write a short story, if not write it for them.

Share marine mammal books, photos and figures with the children. Allow them to explore and play with the figures. Perhaps the marine mammals could be the subject of your stories.

April 28

Celebration: Blueberry Pie Day, Superhero Day

What You Will Need:

Blueberry Pie or ingredients, Superhero clothes or memorabilia

What You'll Do:

If possible make a blueberry pie with the children allowing them to participate as much as you can. If not store-bought what do, enjoy the deliciousness!
For superhero day have the children come dressed as their favorite superhero. Talk about the positive qualities superheroes possess and how we can be more like them.

April 29

Celebration: Zipper Day, World Wish Day, International Dance Day

What You Will Need:

Zippers or zipper frames, International music

What You'll Do:

Use the zipper frames or zippers to demonstrate how to use a zipper. Have the children practice. Talk about the history of zippers and give the proper ncmes for the parts of a zipper.

For International Dance day, provide international music and watch a few dances. Have the children try to replicate what they see. If possible invite a few dancers to class to teach the children a few steps.

Talk about wishes with the children and the superstitions that go along with them. (Wishing on a star, eyelash, birthday candles or dandelions). Give the children an opportunity to talk about their wishes if they want to. Wishes may be a hard concept to grasp, try blowing dandelions or another easily attainable wish getting apparatus.

April 30

Celebration: International Jazz Day, Oatmeal Cookie, Honesty Day

What You Will Need:

Jazz music samples, oatmeal cookies or ingredients to make them

What You'll Do:

Have the children listen to samples of jazz music. Discuss what you hear and the different artists. Perhaps tell a few of their stories. Or, you could discuss some of the songs. If you are able to prepare and bake oatmeal cookies, make them in your classroom. If that's not an option store-bought will do just fine. There are some no bake oatmeal options, too, if you're interested in making them with the children without baking them.
To celebrate Honesty Day, talk to the children about the importance of being honest. Give some examples or scenarios to help them understand the concept. Model the behavior in the classroom.

MAY

MAY

May 1

Celebration: School Principal's Day School Bus Drivers Day, May Day, Mother Goose Day, Global Love Day, Lei Day

What You Will Need:
Thank you notes, treats, Mother Goose books or examples, Lei's, art supplies

What You'll Do:
In keeping with the examples we are setting for appreciation, today we celebrate our Principals and Bus Drivers! We must show the children how much we appreciate the hard work our principals and if applicable, bus drivers, put in each day. Thank you notes, cards or pictures would be a lovely gesture. Treats again, are optional, look to see what you have on hand, investigate your principals favorite things and maybe create a gift basket.

Mother Goose is another childhood staple. Discuss the history of Mother Goose and where some of the rhymes may have come from. Read a few poems to the children, provide examples that they could illustrate. Ask them to memorize a few and maybe take turns reciting their favorites.

Global Love Day sounds like a winner! Show your love for your students by sharing how people show their love across the world. Share traditions and cultures. Or go in a different direction and share love for the planet.

May Day is an oldie but a goodie! This was a favorite of our grandparents, so perhaps invite a few grandparents to helps celebrate. Create a May Pole and sing May Day songs. Enjoy the beautiful weather and take a walk down memory lane.

Lei Day could be a lot of fun, too! Celebrate this day by making lei's with the children. Or use store bought and investigate where lei's are worn and what they symbolize.

There's one thing for sure, there is no shortage of fun on May 1!

Infant/Toddler Adaptation:
If you would like to make cards, stamps and stickers are a great option for small hands.

May 2

Celebration: International Day, Baby Day

What You Will Need:

International foods or cultural items, baby dolls

What You'll Do:

Host an international potluck for your children or invite families from other countries to share their culture items. The possibilities are endless today! Investigate your favorite countries or places the children have visited. Little children love babies! Have a host of baby dolls and talk about the care of babies, sleeping patterns, and how to feed a baby. If you have anyone with a baby brother or sister invite them to come to the room and have mom or dad talk about their experiences with a baby.

Infant/Toddler Adaptation:

Children can participate as you see fit, our young babies love babies

May 3

Celebration: Two Different Colored Shoe Day, Garden Meditation Day

What You Will Need:
Two different colored shoes

What You'll Do:
Ask the children to come to school wearing two different colored shoes. How funny! For Garden Meditation Day, go out to the school garden and just be one with nature! Enjoy the sights and sounds and smells of your schools garden.

Infant/Toddler Adaptation:
Children can participate as you see fit, perhaps skip the different shoes, this happens with these guys without trying. They are learning to match their shoes and to walk and balance, this isn't the best idea for this crew.

May 4

Celebration: Star Wars Day, Firefighters Day, K.I.N.D. (Kids in Needs of Diapers Day)

What You Will Need:
Star Wars clothes, items, thank you notes, diaper drive

What You'll Do:
May the Fourth be with you! Have the children come to school wearing Star Wars clothes, T-shirts or other memorabilia. Celebrate everything from the galaxies far, far away on this fun day!

In keeping with the examples we are setting for appreciation, today we celebrate our local firefighters! We must show the children how much we appreciate the hard work these men and women put in each day. Thank you notes, cards or pictures would be a lovely gesture. Treats again, are optional. You can also invite the firefighters to come to school and visit with the children. Who knows they may be able to bring the fire truck!

K.I.N.D. Day is another way for the children to give back and you can tie this day in with Baby Day from yesterday.

Have the children bring in diapers for babies in need. Check your local organizations for who may have a need.

Infant/Toddler Adaptation:
If you would like to make cards, stamps and stickers are a great option for small hands. The diaper drive may be perfect for outgrown sizes!

May 5

Celebration: Cinco de Mayo Day, Cartoonist Day

What You Will Need:
Cinco de Mayo party items, food, example of cartoons

What You'll Do:
Children will love to celebrate this holiday and there's a lot of things you can do! You can decorate the classroom, share authentic Mexican items or sample authentic Mexican cuisine. Always remember when you celebrate holidays from other cultures to be respectful and avoid any items or food that may not be authentic or could be insulting. We set the example and we want the children to learn about the world around them!

May 6

Celebration: No Homework Day, Beverage Day

What You Will Need:
Beverages

What You'll Do:
If you assign homework- skip it today! Yahoo!
You can take a poll of the children's favorite drinks,
provide the top three at lunch or snack.

May 7

Celebration: Mother's Day

What You Will Need:

Art supplies, card making materials, craft supplies

What You'll Do:

It's time to celebrate Mom. (Be sensitive to those children who may not have mom around or have a non-traditional caretaker situation). Check your craft supplies, any ideas? Mom's love things from their children, but let's face it, macaroni necklaces aren't on the top of the list. Hand or footprint art is sweet. Incorporating photos of the children are also big hits. We want to show our appreciation for our children's moms, too so how about a simple note with some lovely observations about their child? Nothing warms a mother's heart more than hearing nice things about their child.

May 8

Celebration: World Donkey Day, No Socks Day, Iris Day

What You Will Need:
Books, picture and figures of donkeys, Irises

What You'll Do:
Read to the children about donkeys and their habitats and interesting facts about them. Shore photos and allow the children to explore and play with the figures. It's spring time, have the children celebrate No Socks Day by coming in sandals or other shoes with No Socks! Iris Day- is there a more beautiful flower than an iris? Perhaps, but they are such a delightful flower. Have a few for the children to arrange. Or, dissect one and identify all of the parts of a flower.

Infant/Toddler Adaptation:
Children can participate as you see fit, perhaps skip the No Socks if you feel it would be a hinderance.

May 9

Celebration: Europe Day

What You Will Need:
Atlas or Globe

What You'll Do:
Talk with the children about the seven continents. Introduce Europe. Find Europe on your atlas or globe. Discuss the countries in Europe, culture and interesting facts about Europe.

Infant/Toddler Adaptation:
Children can participate

May 10

Celebration: Mother Ocean Day

What You Will Need:
Books, picture and figures of oceans, art supplies

What You'll Do:
Share with the children the books, photos, and any figures of ocean life you may have. If you have been celebrating marine life days throughout the year, you may have some of the books still on hand. If you still have some of the children's art work, perhaps make a large collage of the ocean. If not maybe create a mural for a bulletin board or wall in your room. You can discuss conservation, beach trips, marine life or even ships. Follow the interest of your children and have a blast!

May 11

Celebration: Eat What You Want Day

What You Will Need:
see March 10- Pack Your Own Lunch Day

What You'll Do:
You may be at a school where children pack a lunch every day, if that's the case encourage parents to allow children to choose what goes in their lunch on this particular day. If packing a lunch isn't a typical option this will be an exciting day where children could explore all kinds of lunch options from home. Either way, encourage healthy choices and new and interesting foods!

Infant/Toddler Adaptation:
Children can participate as you see fit, isn't this everyday with this community?

May 12

Celebration: Limerick Day,
International Nurses Day

What You Will Need:
Books and examples of limericks, thank you notes, treats

What You'll Do:
Share with the children the books or examples of limericks you may have.
In keeping with showing our appreciation, today it's for our nurses! We must show the children how much we appreciate the hard work these men and women put in each day. Thank you notes, cards or pictures would be a lovely gesture. Treats again, are optional. You can also invite the nurses to come to school and visit with the children.

Infant/Toddler Adaptation:
If you would like to make cards, stamps and stickers are a great option for small hands.

May 13

Celebration: Numeracy Day,
Frog Jumping Day

What You Will Need:
Numbers!

What You'll Do:
If you have books on numbers, sandpaper numbers, the history of numbers or just anything numbers today is the day to share it! Although we work with numbers frequently in the early childhood classroom, today would be a great day to emphasize or better, *celebrate* numbers! Count everything! Maybe count in other languages, group items, or make numbers with your bodies. There are so many opportunities to celebrate numbers who knows where this day could take you! Play some leap frog for Frog Jumping Day or jump like a frog everywhere you go today! Since we are celebrating numbers, count how many frog jumps you make. Jump!

May 14

Celebration: Chicken Dance Day

What You Will Need:
the chicken dance music, not necessary you know it, you can hum it!

What You'll Do:
Do the chicken dance! Shake your tailfeathers teachers! Everyone loves this dance, share this s lly tradition with your favorite chickies!

Dance!

May 15

Celebration: Chocolate Chip Day, Bring Someone Flowers Day

What You Will Need:
chocolate chips, snacks, flowers

What You'll Do:
Have the children bring snacks that can be topped with chocolate chips in for snack or lunch. Surprise them by providing the chips as toppings for their snack.
Have the class vote on somebody special to bring flowers to and take them to that special person as a class brighten somebody's day!

May 16

Celebration: Drawing Day, Sea Monkey Day

What You Will Need:
art supplies, sea monkeys

What You'll Do:
Have an open ended art day with the children. Celebrate the *art* of just simply drawing. You can provide models, but it's not necessary.
If you can find them, bring some sea monkeys to class explain what they are how they got their name. Give the children time to observe them.

May 17

Celebration: World Baking Day

What You Will Need:
baking supplies and ingredients, toaster oven

What You'll Do:
If you can bake in your class, select a few recipes and have the children help you make some class favorites. If baking is an option then perhaps you could just enjoy some tasty treats from your local bakery. Either way it's a yummy day!

Be mindful of things the children can chew easily.

May 18

Celebration: Museum Day

What You Will Need:
Field trip or video

What You'll Do:
If you were able, take your class on a field trip to a local museum to celebrate museum day. If that's not an option, there are tons of videos that explore museums all over the world. Pick a few and share them with the class. Explain what museums are, what treasures they hold, and why they are so important.

Infant/Toddler Adaptation:
Children can participate as you see fit, perhaps name a few famous pieces of art and have the children repeat.

May 19

Celebration: May flowers

What You Will Need:
art supplies, cupcake papers, pipe cleaners

What You'll Do:
Create an appreciation for flowers by making an art garden. Try cupcake papers for the flowers and pipe cleaners for the stems. Have each child create a few and make a small garden indoors.

Infant/Toddler Adaptation:
Children can participate try putting a picture of each child in the center of each "flower".

May 20

Celebration: Pick Strawberries Day, World Bee Day

What You Will Need:
Field trip, books about bees photos and figures

What You'll Do:
If you are able, take your class on a field trip to pick strawberries. If that's not an option perhaps you could enjoy strawberries in your classroom.
Share with the children books about bees and interesting facts. Allow the children to explore the photos and figures. You could also provide a bit of honey. Yum!

Infant/Toddler Adaptation:
Children can participate as you see fit, honey can not be shared with infants.

May 21

Celebration: Waitstaff Day

What You Will Need:
thank you notes

What You'll Do:
In keeping with showing our appreciation, today it's for our waiters and waitresses! We must show the children how much we appreciate the hard work these men and women put in each day. Thank you notes, cards or pictures would be a lovely gesture. You can also share proper restaurant etiquette and practice how to politely order.

Infant/Toddler Adaptation:
If you would like to make cards, stamps and stickers are a great option for small hands.

May 22

Celebration: Maritime Day

What You Will Need:
maritime books photos or figures

What You'll Do:
Build on what you may have done May 10th. Explore maritime history, depending on what the children are interested in you could talk about oceans, conservancy, the Navy, ships or harbors. There are all sorts of possibilities, let the children guide you as you introduce different topics.

May 23

Celebration: Turtle Day

What You Will Need:

books about turtles photos and figures

What You'll Do:

Share with the children books about turtles and interesting facts. Allow the children to explore the photos and figures.

May 24

Celebration: Brother's Day, Tiara Day

What You Will Need:
photos of brothers, tiaras

What You'll Do:
If the students in your class happen to be a brother, you can share with them how to be a great one! If they happen to have a brother you can share how to treat them well. Give the children opportunities to create artwork depicting their brother, perhaps using photos from home.

It's Tiara Day! The children can come to school wearing a tiara.

Infant/Toddler Adaptation:
If you would like to make cards, stamps and stickers are a great option for small hands.

Infant/Toddler Adaptation:
Children can participate as you see fit, tiaras could be soft.

May 25

Celebration: Tap Dance Day, Towel Day

What You Will Need:
A few short videos showing tap dance routines, towels

What You'll Do:
Share with the children a few short videos showing famous tap dance routines. Allow them to try to re-create what they've seen.

For Towel Day, if the weather is nice and go outside maybe run through the sprinkler! Use the towels to dry off. If it's not quite warm enough yet to get wet, perhaps you could spread your towel out and just have a moment of meditation, yoga or just to sit and look up at the sky. You can also teach the children how to fold their towel!

May 26

Celebration: Paper Airplane Day

What You Will Need:
Paper

What You'll Do:
Help the children make paper airplanes. Have a blast flying them. Adjust your deigns to see if they can go higher/further. Have contests or create awards for most colorful, highest flyer, etc. Try to remember each child for something.

Infant/Toddler Adaptation:
Children can participate as you see fit, have the children go one at a time. Aim away from everyone else.

May 27

Celebration: Sunscreen Day

What You Will Need:
Sunscreen

What You'll Do:
As summer quickly approaches, talk to the children about the importance of sunscreen: how to apply it, how often to apply it, how to reapply it, and how to have an adult help them with sunscreen. Check with local regulations on sunscreen for your school.

Infant/Toddler Adaptation:
Children can participate as you see fit, maybe allowing the children to apply to one area of their body.

May 28

Celebration: Hamburger Day

What You Will Need:
hamburgers, (turkey and veggie if applicable)

What You'll Do:
If you can ask a volunteer to come and grill burgers for your class. If that's not an option, provide hamburgers with all the fixings and talk about America's national food!

May 29

Celebration: Learn About Composting Day, Biscuit (Cookie) Day

What You Will Need:

Books about composting, a compost bin (indoor and outdoor), English biscuits

What You'll Do:

Talk to the children about the importance of composting. If you have a garden, this is an excellent way to help it thrive! Provide a compost bin in your classroom and explain to the children what can and cannot go in to the compost bin. If you have an outdoor compost bin allow the children to empty your classroom bin when it gets full into the outdoor bin. Teach them to turn the compost.

Explain to the children then in England, Biscuit Day is actually celebrating a small English cookie. Provide an authentic English biscuit for the children to sample. You may even be able to provide some tea.

Our little can compost, too. They will need guidance.

May 30

Celebration: Water a Flower Day

What You Will Need:
watering can, flowers

What You'll Do:
Head out to your schools garden with some watering cans or even a hose and water your flowers. Teach the children the importance of being good stewards of the earth today!

May 31

Celebration: Macaroon Day

What You Will Need:
Macaroons

What You'll Do:
Share with the children these yummy treats! Enjoy the sweet deliciousness of a yummy macaroon!

Infant/Toddler Adaptation:
Children can participate as you see fit

JUNE

JUNE

June 1

Celebration: Go Barefoot Day, World Milk Day, Say Something Nice Day

What You Will Need:
Milk

What You'll Do:
Have the children go outside and walk in the grass barefoot. There is nothing more delightful!

Provide some milk for the children if your school doesn't already. If you have access to milk at lunchtime or perhaps snack, talk about the importance of milk. Pair it with some cereal or a cookie, if you are so inclined.
In a world that can seem so negative, let's model how to say something nice. Throughout the day say nice things about everything and everyone we encounter. It will catch on! Have a nice day!

Infants should not have cow's milk.

June 2

Celebration: Rocky Road Day

What You Will Need:
Rocky road ice cream, or ingredients to make traditional Rocky Road (chocolate, peanut butter, nuts, marshmallows)

What You'll Do:
Provide the children with this yummy treat! Mix the ingredients and enjoy or give the children Rocky road ice cream. Either way, it's going to be a delicious day! Be mindful of nut allergies. Make adaptations when necessary.

Infant/Toddler Adaptation:
Children can participate, make adaptations as you see fit.

June 3

Celebration: Repeat Day

What You Will Need:
nothing!

What You'll Do:
Have the children repeat phrases. This can get pretty silly, so expect some giggles! Throw in a tongue twister for good measure!

You can also use motions/actions.

June 4

Celebration: Cheese Day

What You Will Need:
a variety of cheeses-See Jan 20th

What You'll Do:
Provide different variety of cheeses for the children to sample. Discuss where they come from. Discuss how cheese is made. If you celebrated in January, perhaps you could use different cheeses today.

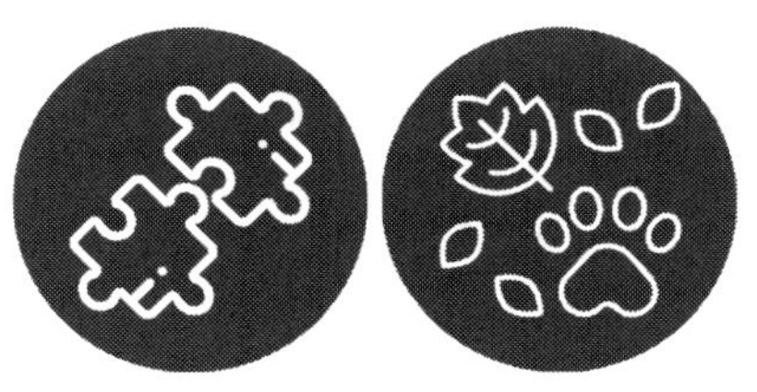

June 5

Celebration: Running Day, World Environment Day, Hot Air Balloon Day

What You Will Need:
athletic shoes, books about the environment, hot air balloons photos and figures, balloons string, small cups

What You'll Do:
For running day, head outside for some good old fashioned races. Try a relay race, hundred yard dash, fifty yard dash or even some sprints. Get creative, try running like your favorite animal!

For World Environment Day, share with the children books about the environment or conservation talk about what you're already doing in your classroom and think of ideas of ways to do more.

For hot air balloon day, share book, photos and figures of hot air balloons. Create some beautiful artwork with hot air balloons as a theme. Or use balloons, string and paper cups to fashion hot air balloons of your own.

This group may not need structured races. Maybe set up a small "course" with cones or follow a short trail.

Gluing designs (jewels, strips of paper- whatever you may have) onto a pre-cut hot air balloon may be a nice adaptation.

June 6

Celebration: Yo-yo Day, Gardening Exercise Day, Drive-in Movie Day

What You Will Need:
Yo-yo's

What You'll Do:
Have the children bring in yo-yos or provide a few yo-yos and let the children explore different yo-yo techniques. For Gardening Exercise Day, head out to the garden for a few fun stretches. Try to be as straight and tall as a carrot or sunflower. Maybe even incorporate pulling weeds as an exercise.

Let's all head to the movies! Drive-in movie day could be so much fun! Collect boxes that are large enough for children to sit in them. Design a car for the outer part of the box, complete with paper headlights and tires, have the children "drive-in" to the movie. Provide popcorn and other movie treats!

Infant/Toddler Adaptation:
Children can participate as you see fit, yo-yo's may be a bit hard to use, maybe do some demo's.

June 7

Celebration: Chocolate Ice Cream Day, VCR Day

What You Will Need:
Chocolate ice cream, VCR

What You'll Do:
Provide some delicious chocolate ice cream for the children. Have them top it with all kinds of fruit to make a healthier treat.
For VCR day if you can locate a VCR bring it in and explain to the children how it works. It may be a history lesson!

Infant/Toddler Adaptation:
Children can participate, you could sub a chocolate avocado mash recipe for ice cream if it's a concern. Children under three shouldn't really have screen time. If you participated in the drive-in yesterday, consider skipping the VCR Day altogether.

June 8

Celebration: World Ocean's Day, Upsy Daisy Day (positive day), Best Friends Day

What You Will Need:
Books, picture and figures of oceans, art supplies

What You'll Do:
If you weren't able celebrate May 10th or if you did you can continue to expand on this topic. Share with the children the books, photos, and any figures of ocean life you may have. If you have been celebrating marine life days throughout the year, you may have some of the books still on hand. If you still have some of the children's art work, perhaps make a large collage of the ocean. If not maybe create a mural for a bulletin board or wall in your room. You can discuss conservation, beach trips, marine life or even ships. Follow the interest of your children and have a blast!

Upsy Daisy Day sounds like fun! Basically, you just need to be positive. If you want to give the children a visual cue, you could use a daisy as you say or do something positive. Or have the children think of nice things about staff and faculty members. Write them on slips of paper and attach to daisies. Have the children deliver them. Best Friends Day could be a bit tricky. We all know that everyone is the young child's best friend.

We also know a lot of the time, this changes day to day. To avoid hurt feelings or someone getting left out, maybe spin this into how to be the *best* friend you can be. We should foster the real relationships children are forming by encouraging them to be a good friend.

Upsy Daisy means something completely different for this group, so maybe just being your sweet, positive self today will do. No need for labels.

June 9

Celebration: Donald Duck Day

What You Will Need:

Videos showing Donald Duck, cartoons

What You'll Do:

Show the children the videos, have them try to talk like the famous duck.

Infant/Toddler Adaptation:

Children can participate perhaps a short video or audio recording and some Donald art would work.

June 10

Celebration: Herds and Spices Day

What You Will Need:
Books, photos and examples of herb and spices

What You'll Do:
Read the books and share the photos and examples of herbs and spices with the children. If you have herbs growing in your garden, visit the garden and investigate. Allow the children to smell the herbs and spices- if possible allow them to sample them.

June 11

Celebration: Corn Cob Day

What You Will Need:

Corn on the cob

What You'll Do:

have the children help you shuck the corn peel all of the thread and prepare the corn for boiling or roasting. If possible cook the corn in your classroom if not try to have it prepared off site and then enjoy hot, delicious corn on the cob.

Infant/Toddler Adaptation:

Children can participate, they may need help. Allow them to hold, smell and peel the corn before preparing regardless of whether or not they will eat it.

June 12

Celebration: Superman Day

What You Will Need:
Superman clothing

What You'll Do:
Have the children dress in their Superman best. Discuss Superman, his history, author and redeeming qualities. Ask the children how they can be "super". Have a "super" day!

June 13

Celebration: Weed the Garden Day

What You Will Need:
Gardening gloves, tools

What You'll Do:
Head out to the garden to help tend to it. Help the children identify weeds vs plants that should be there. Explain the importance of caring for the plants.

June 14

Celebration: Flag Day, International Bath Day, Cupcake Day

What You Will Need:

An American flag, books about the history of Flag Day, Bubbles, bubble bath, large washtub, swimsuits, cupcakes

What You'll Do:

Share with the children the history of the Flag and it's symbolism. You can incorporate patriotic songs. You could have flag cupcakes!

Bath time may not be possible at school, but preparing for a bubble bath when the children get home could be fun. Perhaps making a small bit of bubble bath for later would be a fun project. The weather may permit for some fun "baths" outdoors. Fill a washtub full of water and bubble bath. Have the children suit up in swimsuits and dive in. The rule is- the more bubbles the better! Children not splashing in the tub could be blowing or chasing bubbles.

Once the children are all clean they can have a cupcake and the fun can start all over again.

Infant/Toddler Adaptation:
Children can participate, blowing bubbles is an alternative the children are sure to love.

June 15

Celebration: Smile Power Day, Nature Photography Day

What You Will Need:
smiles and a camera, examples of great nature photos

What You'll Do:
Talk to the children about the power of a smile and how a simple smile can change the course of the day. Encourage children to smile and you'll see how happy your classroom can be!

For Nature Photography Day have the children had outside with a camera. Let them practice taking some pictures of nature. Record who took each picture and display their work.

Infant/Toddler Adaptation:
Children can participate, they may need some help with the camera.

June 16

Celebration: Fresh Veggies Day

What You Will Need:

fresh veggies

What You'll Do:

Provide a variety of fresh veggies for the children to sample. Try to include some less common ones that they may not have tried or a few exotic varieties. Provide dips if you like.

Infant/Toddler Adaptation:

Children can participate, you may need to cook or mash for our young friends.

June 17

Celebration: Eat Your Vegetables Day

What You Will Need:
Vegetables from yesterday

What You'll Do:
Use any veggies from yesterday to continue this healthy eating streak!

Infant/Toddler Adaptation:
Children can participate, you may need to cook or mash for our young friends.

June 18

Celebration: International Picnic Day, International Sushi Day

What You Will Need:
Picnic baskets, blankets and picnic foods, sushi

What You'll Do:
Talk to the children about what a picnic is and what you'll need to make a great picnic. Prepare your picnic baskets, fold up your blankets, and head outside for a lovely group picnic. Enjoy all kinds of goodies and eating outdoors!

You could incorporate sushi into your picnic menu, but since it's not a typical picnic food, you may want to introduce it separately. If you want to celebrate International Sushi Day, try a few varieties. Avoid raw sushi in school.

Infant/Toddler Adaptation:
Children can participate, make food adaptations where you see fit.

June 19

Celebration: Wear Blue Day

What You Will Need:

Blue Clothing

What You'll Do:

Have the children come to school dressed in blue. Talk about all the different shades of blue and try to name them.

June 20

Celebration: American Eagle Day, Ice Cream Soda Day, Vanilla Milkshake Day

What You Will Need:
Books, photos and figures of American Eagles. Vanilla ice cream, soda (you can get caffeine-free), milk, a blender

What You'll Do:
Share with the children the books, photos, and any figures of American Eagles you may have. Discuss the significance of our national bird.

You can combine Ice Cream Soda and Vanilla Milkshake Day and for a delicious treat. Make them both and let the children vote on their favorite. Or, have the children choose which one they would like. Either way, you can't go wrong!

Infant/Toddler Adaptation:
Children can participate, make food adaptations where you see fit.

June 21

Celebration: World Music Day, Skateboard Day, Daylight Appreciation Day

What You Will Need:

Samples of music from around the world, skateboards, pads

What You'll Do:

Play the children samples of the music from around the world. Listen for specific instruments, different languages, and different rhythms. Enjoy!
You may want to skip Skateboard Day. But if you are feeling adventurous, provide a few skateboards and pads and help the children navigate their way on a skateboard. If you can locate a proficient skateboarder, if may be fun to have them come by and demonstrate a few moves for the children.

While your outside, take a few moments to appreciate the daylight!

Infant/Toddler Adaptation:

Children can participate, skip the skateboarding, maybe just name the skateboard and it's parts.

June 22

Celebration: World Rainforest Day

What You Will Need:
Books, photos and materials to create your own rainforest

What You'll Do:
Share with the children in the books and photos of the rainforest. Discuss the animals and plants that you can find there. Allow the children to explore the materials you provided. Look through your art supplies and craft supplies and work with the children to create a group project recreating the rainforest.

Infant/Toddler Adaptation:
Children can participate as you see fit, perhaps you could provide figures of animals from the rainforest for naming and explorative play.

June 23

Celebration: Public Service Day, Typewriter Day, Let it Go Day

What You Will Need:

Thank you notes, typewriter, a recording of the song "Let It Go"

What You'll Do:

Speak with the children about appreciating those in public service. Identify your local public servants and create thank you notes and maybe treats for them. Or invite them into your classroom to speak with the children.

If you can locate a typewriter bring it in for the children to type on. The children practice typing their name or other words/phrases they may know. You could type a sweet message to each of them ahead of time and give it to them as a surprise.

Talk to the children about the importance of letting things go. If you are brave, you could play the song from the famous Disney movie to emphasize your point. Be prepared to hear the song the rest of the day.

Infant/Toddler Adaptation:

If you would like to make cards, stamps and stickers are a great option for small hands. While the typewriter may appeal to the small child, they are probably not quite ready to use it appropriately. If you want to share one with the children. Consider naming the typewriter and all of it's parts.

June 24

Celebration: Fairy Day, Upcycling Day

What You Will Need:

Books, photos and figures of fairies, items to upcycle

What You'll Do:

If you choose to celebrate Fairy Day, remind the children that they are fantasy characters. Children are trying to order their world, so it's important to mention it. You can keep the day magical by sharing pictures, creating art projects or creating stories about fairies. Fairy houses are lovely ways to do this.

Check your supplies and determine what you can upcycle. Perhaps you have things that you could turn into fairy houses! Explain the importance of reusing items with the children.

June 25

Celebration: Global Beatles Day, Catfish Day

What You Will Need:
Beatles Music, books, photos and figures of catfish

What You'll Do:
If you haven't already, share some of your favorite Beatles tunes with the children. Teach them a few songs, or play the music in the background throughout the day. Provide books, photos or figures of catfish. Share interesting facts about them.

Infant/Toddler Adaptation:
Children can participate.

June 26

Celebration: Chocolate Pudding Day, Beautician's Day, Canoe Day

What You Will Need:

Chocolate pudding, thank you notes, a canoe

What You'll Do:

Provide some chocolate pudding for the children to sample. You can make it or use store-bought. Enjoy! Speak with the children about appreciating those in who work to make us beautiful and handsome. Create thank you notes and maybe treats for them. Or invite them into your classroom to speak with the children and discuss what they do. You can also use this time to talk about getting a haircut, which can be scary, and how to behave when visiting a salon or barbershop. (Be mindful that this discussion may spark in one of the children the notion to cut their own hair or worse a friend's! Watch over your scissors closely for a few days).

If you can get a canoe to school, how much fun could you have! The children could pile in and you go on "adventures". Teach then camp songs or how to paddle. Just have a blast!

Infant/Toddler Adaptation:

If you would like to make cards, stamps and stickers are a great option for small hands.

June 27

<hr>

Celebration: Sunglasses Day

What You Will Need:
sunglasses

What You'll Do:
We wear our sunglasses to school! Have the children wear their sunglasses to class. Discuss the importance of protecting their eyes in the sun. Be cool.

Infant/Toddler Adaptation:
Children can participate.

June 28

Celebration: Happy Heart Hugs Day, Tapioca Day

What You Will Need:

tapioca pudding

What You'll Do:

Give hugs! Make some little hearts happy! Let's also use this as a time to teach children about boundaries and asking to hug someone before touching them. Teaching children that they don't have to hug if they don't want to may seem like a downer on such a joyful day, but it's an important grace and courtesy lesson that can be invaluable to our young friends.

Provide some tapioca pudding for the children to sample. You can make it with the children, or use store-bought. What a great day!

Infant/Toddler Adaptation:

Children can participate.

June 29

Celebration: Camera Day, International Mud Day, Waffle Iron Day

What You Will Need:

Camera, mud puddles, changes of clothes, waffle ingredients, a waffle iron

What You'll Do:

Provide a few examples of cameras if you have them. Discuss how they have changed over time. Allow the children to take photos and display their work. Name the parts of the camera and have the children identify them.

Head outside and find a big mud puddle. If you can't find one, make one. Make sure the children are wearing mud-appropriate clothing. Splash, make mud pies, and mud sculptures. Rinse off and change if necessary.

Who doesn't love waffles? Bring out the waffle iron and get cooking! Encourage the children to participate as much as possible in your classroom. Children can mix the batter, pour into the waffle maker, apply fruit toppings and whip cream, if applicable. Waffles are delicious and you can discuss their origin and history while you're preparing them.

If cooking is not an option in your classroom, you could choose already prepared waffles and incorporate those into your lesson. When we cook with the children we should always model hygienic practices and when we eat with the children we should a ways model appropriate eating habits. Children are always looking to us to set a good example.

Infant/Toddler Adaptation:
Children can participate, make adaptations where you see fit.

June 30

Celebration: Log Cabin Day

What You Will Need:

Lincoln Logs

What You'll Do:

Gather the children and have them create a log cabin village. This will take many logs, so gather several sets. While you are building, discuss the history of log cabins.

Infant/Toddler Adaptation:

Children can participate.

JULY

JULY

July 1

Celebration: Canada Day, International Joke Day, International Reggae Day, Postal Worker Day

What You Will Need:

Map or Globe, Books or photos about Canada, Joke books, Samples of Reggae Music, Thank you notes, treats

What You'll Do:

Read the books and share the photos of Canada. Look on the globe or atlas and have the children locate Canada. Discuss customs and traditions and how Canada day is celebrated.

Share jokes with the children.

Play samples of reggae music. Discuss the history of reggae music. Let children listen for different instruments. Show your appreciation for postal workers by writing thank you notes and/or making treats for all of their hard work making sure the mail is always delivered on time. Infant/Toddler Adaptation: Children can participate as you see fit, perhaps avoiding any jokes today, they make not "get" them. If you would like to make cards, stamps and stickers are a great option for small hands.

July 2

Celebration: Red, White and Blue Day

What You Will Need:
Red, white and blue clothing

What You'll Do:
Chances are you will not be in session for the 4th. Celebrate a bit early by having the children come dressed in red, white and blue. Have red, white and blue balloons, snacks, and décor. Use what you have on hand if possible. Discuss the significance of the colors with the children.

July 3

Celebration: Eat Beans Day, Disobedience Day

What You Will Need:

A variety of beans

What You'll Do:

Provide a variety of beans for the children to sample. Teach them the names and discuss the differences. Disobedience is not something to celebrate. Instead try talking to the children about trying not to be disobedient. Put a positive spin on any naughty behaviors you may have noticed in the classroom.

Our young friends may not understand disobedience, so modeling a few desired behaviors may work better.

July 4

Celebration: Independence Day

What You Will Need:

American items- (flag, songs, symbols)

What You'll Do:

Introduce the children to the history of Independence Day. Share the symbols and meanings of things they may see or hear. You could color the American flag, sing patriotic songs, or make a patriotic craft. You could also make a yummy treat, maybe a red, white and blue treat- berry parfaits, or maybe hotdog or mini sliders.

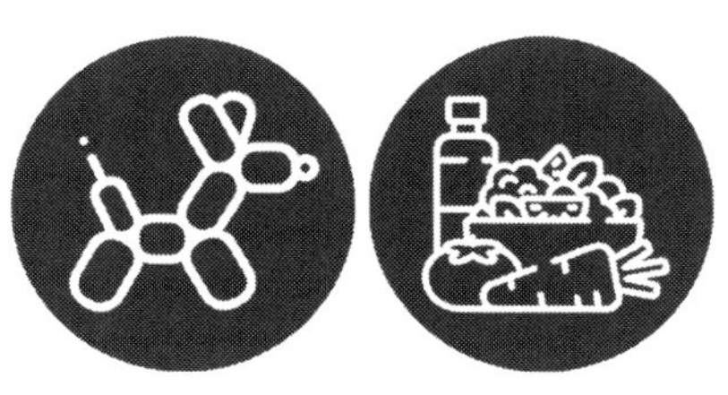

July 5

Celebration: Mechanical Pencil Day, Apple Turnover Day

What You Will Need:

Mechanical pencils, apple turnovers or ingredients to make them

What You'll Do:

Celebrate something that delights all young children… mechanical pencils. We all remember how much fun it was to use them, now let's pass that love on to our children! This also a great way to promote writing. How much fun can writing be with a mechanical pencil? Apple turnovers are a delicious American favorite! You can prepare them with the children or if that's not possible enjoy some store-bought turnovers. Yum!

Infant/Toddler Adaptation:

Children can participate as you see fit, skip the mechanical pencils if your students aren't ready to use them.

July 6

Celebration: Fried Chicken Day

What You Will Need:
fried chicken

What You'll Do:
As much fun as cooking with the children can be, preparing fried chicken may be a bit too dangerous. Enjoy some prepared chicken with the children, you could even head outside for a fried chicken picnic!

Infant/Toddler Adaptation:
Children can participate as you see fit, chicken should be cut off the bone if you decide your students could participate.

July 7

Celebration: Tell the Truth Day, Global Forgiveness Day, Strawberry Sundae Day

What You Will Need:

Strawberry ice cream, whipped cream, strawberries, strawberry syrup

What You'll Do:

Discuss the importance of telling the truth with the children. You can role play to help them understand the concept.

Helping children understand forgiveness is a very important part of our work. You can tie the is in with Tell the Truth Day. Role playing is helpful for small children to understand these complex concepts.

Help the children make a delicious treat! Scoop out strawberry ice cream and top with fresh strawberries, whipped cream or strawberry syrup. Enjoy!

Infant/Toddler Adaptation:

Children can participate as you see fit, this group may have a hard time with the concepts of truth and forgiveness. Perhaps practicing saying "I'm sorry" would be a good adaptation.

July 8

Celebration: Math 2.0 Day

What You Will Need:

Math and technology

What You'll Do:

If you have access to technology, download an app or demonstrate how math and technology have meshed over the years. Keep screen time to a minimum, but enjoy it.

Skip the screens and introduce numbers to the children.

July 9

Celebration: Sugar Cookie Day

What You Will Need:
Ingredients to make sugar cookies or store bought cookies

What You'll Do:
Prepare the cookies with the children, or use store bought. If you want, ice the cookies or add sprinkles. The children could make designs or practice writing the first letter of the name.

July 10

Celebration: Teddy Bear Picnic Day, Don't Step on a Bee Day

What You Will Need:
Teddy bears, picnic supplies

What You'll Do:
Have the children bring food for a picnic and their favorite teddy bear. Teach them the teddy bears picnic song. Head outside and enjoy!

Even though the theme is a bit specific, you can still use today to talk about the importance of bees and we must all work together to protect them.

July 11

Celebration: Blueberry Muffin Day

What You Will Need:

Blueberry muffin mix or store bought muffins

What You'll Do:

Mix the ingredients together and bake the muffins with the children. If you aren't able to cook in your room, enjoy some prepared muffins!

July 12

Celebration: Pecan Pie Day, Etch a Sketch Day

What You Will Need:
Etch a Sketches

What You'll Do:
If you are able to have nuts, you can prepare pecan pies with the children or enjoy a prepared pie. Look for the mini one for a sweet snack!
Show the children how to use an Etch-a- Sketch. Let them explore and create designs.

Infant/Toddler Adaptation:
Children can participate as you see fit, if you celebrate Pecan Pie Day be mindful of nut allerg es and choking issues.

July 13

Celebration: International Rock Day, Learn about French Fries Day

What You Will Need:
Books, pictures and examples of rocks, French fries

What You'll Do:
Read the books an share the photos and examples of rocks with the children. Name the different rocks and invite the children to explore the rocks.
Enjoy French fries with the children as you share the history and fun fry facts. Like: did you know French fries originated in Belgium and *not* France?

July 14

Celebration: Mac & Cheese Day, Shark Awareness Day

What You Will Need:

Books, pictures and examples of sharks, Mac & Cheese

What You'll Do:

Read the books an share the photos and examples of sharks with the children. Name the different types of sharks and invite the children to explore the figures and photos of the sharks.

Enjoy an all time childhood favorite, Mac & Cheese, with the children. Whether you are able to prepare it in the classroom or enjoy prepared deliciousness, you are sure to have a group of happy children!

July 15

Celebration: Tapioca Pudding Day, Gummy Worm Day

What You Will Need:

Tapioca Pudding (or ingredients) and Gummy Worms

What You'll Do:

Two sweet celebrations in one day! Enjoy tapioca pudding with the children. And, top it off with gummy worms. You can discuss how each decadent dessert is made.

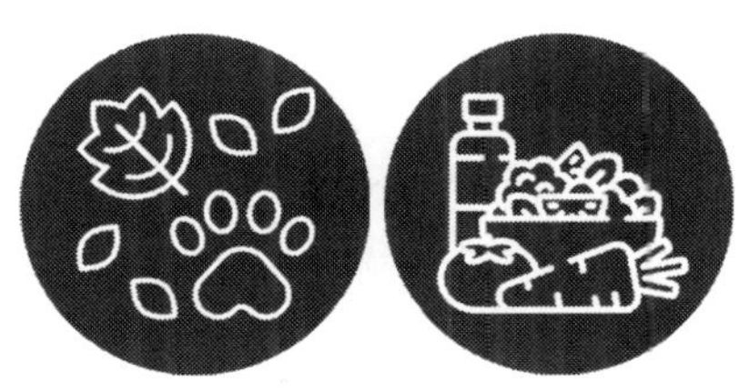

July 16

Celebration: World Snake Day, Guinea Pig Appreciation Day, Fresh Spinach Day

What You Will Need:
Books, photos, and figures of snakes and guinea pigs, fresh spinach

What You'll Do:
Read the books an share the photos and examples of sharks with the children. Discuss the habitats and interesting facts. Name the different sharks and invite the children to explore and play with the figures.
You can do the same for guinea pigs. If you happen to have a guinea pig as a class pet, throw a party for your friend! Have the children bring treats for your pet.
For Fresh Spinach Day, provide the chidren with fresh spinach to sample. If you want to get fancy, make fresh spinach salads or add some to wraps.

July 17

Celebration: Peach Ice Cream Day, Tattoo Day

What You Will Need:

Peach Ice Cream, temporary tattoos, parent permission.

What You'll Do:

Provide the children with some delicious peach ice cream, add fresh peaches for an even sweeter treat. Check with your school and the policies before celebrating Tattoo Day. If you decide to celebrate, you will probably also need parent permission. You can provide temporary tattoos for the children to choose from. Help them apply them. You can discuss the history or tattoos and show the children pictures and examples of exceptional ones.

July 18

Celebration: Mandela Day

What You Will Need:

Books, pictures and short videos

What You'll Do:

Introduce Nelson Mandela and talk about his life with the children. Maybe you could plan some good deeds for the children. Talk with the children and brainstorm with them for ideas. You may be surprised what they come up with after hearing about Mandela's life.

July 19

Celebration: Water Balloon Day

What You Will Need:

Tons of water balloons, changes of clothes

What You'll Do:

Fill up a bunch of water balloons and head outside for some old fashioned fun. Ensure that no one gets hurts by organizing a few games rather than a free for all.
Let the children feel the balloons and maybe throw them at a target.

July 20

Celebration: Lollipop Day, Space Explorations Day, Moon Day, World Jump Day

What You Will Need:

Lollipops, Books, pictures and short videos or figures of space ships and the moon

What You'll Do:

Provide the children with lollipops. You can talk about the flavors, the origin of lollipops, or if you are really adventurous, make your own lollipops with the children! Read the books an share the photos and examples of spacecrafts with the children. Discuss the history of space travel and interesting facts. Name the different ships and invite the children to explore and play with the figures. You can also include discussions about the moon.

It's World Jump Day! Jump for joy! Jump wherever you going throughout the school. See how high or far you can jump. Have the best time jumping with the children! Lollipops may be a choking hazard.

July 21

Celebration: Junk Food Day

What You Will Need:
A collection of junk food, or healthy alternatives

What You'll Do:
You can either pig out today, or use today to teach children about healthy alternatives to some of their favorite junk food treats.

July 22

Celebration: Mango Day, Hammock Day

What You Will Need:

Mangoes, Hammocks

What You'll Do:

Give the children fresh mangoes to sample. If you are
feeling adventurous, look for mango recipes to try.
If you have access to hammocks, set up a few and let
the children test them out.

Watch the children around hammocks. Different models
may have rope/string that could be choking hazards.

July 23

Celebration: Peanut Butter and Chocolate Day, Sprinkler Day

What You Will Need:

Peanut butter and chocolate, sprinklers, swim suits and towels

What You'll Do:

Provide the children with peanut butter and chocolate, maybe use Reese's peanut butter cups or Reese's pieces. (Be mindful of peanut allergies).
Have the children bring swimsuits and towels and head out side for some water play! Set up several sprinklers and let the children run through them and have some summer fun. Remember to follow sunscreen policy and procedures.

July 24

Celebration: Cousins Day, Pioneer Day

What You Will Need:

Cousin info, books about family, Books and stories about pioneers and their lives, any educational aids that represent pioneers

What You'll Do:

Discuss families and how cousins are re ated to us. Use the info you gathered about the children's cousins and help them create pictures or cards for their cousins. Read the books and/or stories about pioneers. Discuss interesting facts and historical figures. Share with the children any aids you may have.

July 25

Celebration: Hot Fudge Sundae, Thread a Needle Day, Carousel Day

What You Will Need:

Hot fudge sundae ingredients, Needle and thread (there are some great plastic beginner needles for children who have not sewn before) Field trip to a carousel

What You'll Do:

Prepare hot fudge sundaes with the children. Allow them to help as much as possible. Scoop out ice cream and top with hot fudge, nuts (if possible), whipped cream and a cherry. Perfect for summer!

Allow the children to try their hand a sewing. Teach them how to thread a needle and maybe go a step further and help them sew a few stitches or a button. Handiwork is becoming a lost art, help the children build hand-eye coordination and concentration by introducing sewing to your students.

If you have a carousel in your area, maybe a field trip would be a perfect way to spend Carousel Day. If not, books or photos would work. Discuss the craftmanship, animals of other figures that appear on the carousel, or the history of carousels with the children.

July 26

Celebration: Aunt & Uncle Day

What You Will Need:

Aunt & Uncle info

What You'll Do:

Use the info you gathered about the children's aunts and uncles to create cards or pictures for them. Discuss family relations and how aunts and uncles fit in on the family tree.

July 27

Celebration: Chicken Finger Day, Take Your Houseplant for a Walk Day

What You Will Need:

Chicken fingers, dips, houseplants

What You'll Do:

Provide chicken fingers for the children. You can prepare them in the classroom or use prepared chicken fingers. Children love chicken fingers, so they have probably tried them before. To make it interesting, provide a variety of sauces for the children to sample.

Take Your Houseplant for a Walk Day is a bit silly and even though the children may find it hilarious, it probably would not work out so well for your classroom plants. You could use this day to discuss the proper care of a houseplant. Children will see the humor in this day without actually walking around with the plants. You can name or identify the plants and it's parts.

July 28

Celebration: Milk Chocolate Day

What You Will Need:
Milk chocolate

What You'll Do:
Have a delicious day eating milk chocolate. To make it a bit healthier, cover fruits, nuts or granola in milk chocolate. Either way, enjoy!

July 29

Celebration: Learn About Rain Day, Lasagna Day, International Tiger Day

What You Will Need:

Books, photos and figures of tigers, rain or the water cycle and lasagna

What You'll Do:

Read the books an share the photos and examples of the water cycle with the children. Discuss rain and interesting facts. If you happen to have a rainy day, head outside to investigate!

Preparing a lasagna is intense, so sharing a prepared one while discussing how they are made and the ingredients used is probably your best bet. Lasagnas are delicious and there is so much to talk about. We must follow the children's conversation and as always, model manners as we enjoy this treat!

Read the books an share the photos and examples of tigers with the children. Discuss the habitats and interesting facts. Name the different tigers and invite the children to explore and play with the figures.

July 30

Celebration: Paperback Book Day, Cheesecake Day, Share a Hug Day

What You Will Need:
Paperback books (hardback to show the contrast), Cheesecake (bites would work well today)

What You'll Do:
Introduce paperback books, show a hardback book to illustrate the difference. Allow the children to peruse the paperback books and read them.

Provide cheesecake for the children today. Cheesecake bites would be ideal, because they would be the ideal serving size for such a rich dessert.

We have celebrated several days that involve hugs, and Share a Hug Day is no different. These might be the best days ever! As always, let's use this as a time to teach children about boundaries and asking to hug someone before touching them. Teaching children that they don't have to hug if they don't want to may seem like a downer on such a joyful day, but it's an important grace and courtesy lesson that can be invaluable to our young friends.

July 31

Celebration: Uncommon Instrument Day, World Ranger Day, Raspberry Cake Day

What You Will Need:

Short recordings or videos of uncommon instruments, thank you notes, treats, Raspberry cake

What You'll Do:

Share recordings or videos of uncommon instruments. If these instruments happen to be from another culture, we must remember to be respectful. Just because they are uncommon does not mean they aren't amazing. We must convey this to the children by modeling respect and awe.

Make thank you notes for local park ranger in your area thanking them for all their hard work. If possible, invite them to the classroom to speak with the children. Provide treats if you like.

Provide raspberry cake to the children to celebrate this sweet day.

AUGUST

AUGUST

August 1

Celebration: Respect for Parents Day, Rounds Resounding Day

What You Will Need:
Nothing!

What You'll Do:
Talk to the children about being respectful toward their parents. Remember, we are modeling behavior for them, so we must be respectful toward their parents as well. Role play is always helpful, of sharing personal stories or a book may help they children understand.

Singing in rounds is super fun! It may take a few tries for the children to get the hang of it, but stick with it, the end result is the best!

Singing in rounds is going to be a bit much for this group, so consider sharing recordings of other folks singing in rounds.

August 2

Celebration: Coloring Book Day, Ice Cream Sandwich Day

What You Will Need:

Coloring books, crayons, ice cream sandwiches

What You'll Do:

Provide the children with a variety of coloring books and crayons. Even though we hear so much about coloring outside the lines, coloring inside the lines is a great tool for hand- eye coordination and pencil control, so don't knock it. You can also have the children draw pictures and have friends color them, creating their own coloring books.

Share ice cream sandwiches with the children for a yummy, easy summer treat!

August 3

Celebration: Watermelon Day

What You Will Need:
Watermelon

What You'll Do:
Share watermelon with the children. You can get creative and carve figures or animals in the watermelon or just cut up some slices and enjoy!

August 4

Celebration: Coast Guard Day

What You Will Need:
Thank you notes, treats

What You'll Do:
Explain to the children what the Coast Guard is and what they do. Have the children make cards or treats to send to the men and women who are serving.

August 5

Celebration: Work Like a Dog Day, Underwear Day

What You Will Need:
Pictures of or books about breeds of dogs in the working group, Sample underwear

What You'll Do:
Teach children about dog breeds and why certain dogs are considered "working dogs". Also show examples of dogs that have jobs (military/police dogs, dog actors, search & rescue dogs, service/therapy/support animals, farm dogs, and even dogs that work at the zoo!) You can show pictures and videos of these dogs doing their important jobs.

Talking about underwear may be an awkward or sensitive subject. This is a tricky one, so proceed with a bit of caution (and definitely give parents a heads up!) You can discuss the importance of underwear. Maybe how to make sure you are wearing it right. Or, show the children pictures of historical underclothes that are guaranteed to make them laugh.

Infant/Toddler Adaptation:
Children can participate as you see fit, potty-training children are the perfect target audience for discussing the importance of underwear.

August 6

Celebration: Wiggle Your Toes Day, Root beer Float Day, Farm Worker Appreciation Day

What You Will Need:
Thank you notes or treats, Root beer float- ingredients

What You'll Do:
Well, of course you can celebrate wiggling your toes. How much fun is that?

Provide the children with the ingredients to make root beer floats. Allow them to make them.

Discuss with the children the importance of farm workers and how their work affects each of us. Have the children make cards or treats to send to your local farmers and farm workers.

August 7

Celebration: Lighthouse Day

What You Will Need:

Books, pictures and examples or figures of light houses
What You'll Do: Read the books, share the photos and
figure of lighthouses. Allow the children to explore and
play with them.

August 8

Celebration: Bowling Day, Cat Day

What You Will Need:
Bowling pins & ball, cat books, photos and figures
What You'll Do: Set up bowling games for the children to play with.

Read the books and share photos of different breeds of cats. You can also talk about any cats the children may have as pets.

August 9

Celebration: Rice Pudding Day, Melon Day, Book Lovers Day

What You Will Need:
Rice pudding, melons, a variety of books

What You'll Do:
Provide rice pudding and/or a variety of melons for the children to sample. You can talk about the different varieties of melons with the children.

Talk with the children about ow much you love to read and love books. Although it won't happen in one day, we must foster the child's love of reading. Today is a great day to start.

August 10

Celebration: World Lion Day, Skyscraper Appreciation Day, S'mores Day

What You Will Need:
Books, photos and figures of lions, skyscrapers, ingredients to make s'mores. You probably cannot have an open flame, so ready-made s'mores might be the way to go today.

What You'll Do:
Read to the children about lions, talk about the habitats and interesting facts you discover. Share the pictures and figures, allow the children to play and explore.
Read book, share photos and discuss skyscrapers. Look and see what you may have on hand to build a few as a group.

Show the children how to assemble a traditional s'more. Get creative on how you will heat the marshmallows. Look for prepackages s'mores if cooking is an issue.

August 11

Celebration: Play in the Sand Day, Son/Daughter Day

What You Will Need:
Sand, sand toys, Letter to parents

What You'll Do:
Head outside for some fun in the sand! If you already have a sandbox, try sprucing it up, add new sand, colored sand, or new toys and tools for the children to use. If you are starting from scratch, you can do the same things, just make sure you have plenty of sand for the children to play in. Today may be the day to ask a volunteer or two to help build a sandbox. Check with local guideline on sand use and storage.

For Son/Daughter day, you may want to send a letter home to parents. Explain the day. You could invite them to have lunch with the children. Or perhaps they could send in letters, cards or photos as a surprise for the children. Whatever you choose, help the parents express the love for the children and help the children to feel like a loved son or daughter today.

August 12

Celebration: International Youth Day, World Elephant Day, Vinyl Record Day

What You Will Need:

Party/celebration items, Books, photos and figures of elephants, record player, records

What You'll Do:

Celebrate International Youth day with a party or carnival! Have a bounce house or face painters. Enjoy all kinds of treats. The sky is the limit! Have fun and celebrate our sweet students!

Read books, discuss their habitats and the difference between n Asian and African elephants. Share phots and figure of elephants with the children. Allow them to play and explore.

If you can obtain one, bring in a record player for the children. Play a few records. Allow the children to hear the awesome sounds vinyl makes.

Name the parts of the record player and records.

August 13

Celebration: Lefthanders Day

What You Will Need:
Nothing!

What You'll Do:
Discuss with the children handedness. Talk about the different preferences.

This may be a day to skip.

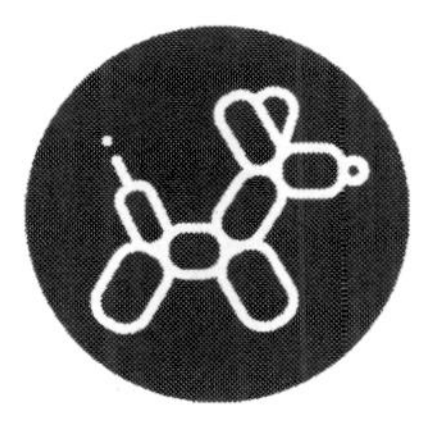

August 14

Celebration: Back to School Day

What You Will Need:
Books about the first day of school

What You'll Do:
Although this may not be the first day of school for you, children are gearing up to head to school or return to the classroom. Talk to them about what they may experience. Help them become excited about school!

Adapt for your age group.

August 15

Celebration: Lemon Meringue Pie Day

What You Will Need:
Lemon meringue pie or ingredients to make one

What You'll Do:
Lemon meringue pie is the best! Help the children prepare one or use store bought if that's not an option for you. Meringue is actually not too difficult to make, so maybe having the children make just the meringue would be happy compromise today.

August 16

Celebration: Tell a Joke Day

What You Will Need:

Joke books, jokes

What You'll Do:

By now, you should have quite the collection of jokes. Tell a few favorites, look for some new knee-slappers. We must remember that laughter is so important for our young ones. Enjoy the day!

August 17

Celebration: Vanilla Custard Day

What You Will Need:

Vanilla Custard or ingredients to make it

What You'll Do:

Make a delicious vanilla custard with the children, or use one that's been prepared. Either way it's going to be a scrumptious day!

August 18

Celebration: Serendipity Day

What You Will Need:
Nothing

What You'll Do:
Serendipity may be a bit difficult to explain, but isn't that what makes it wonderful. We know days in the classroom can be pleasantly unexpected. Try to emphasize this today in the best ways.

August 19

Celebration: Aviation Day, Potato Day, International Bow Day

What You Will Need:

Books, pictures and figure of things that fly, Baked Potatoes, Bows

What You'll Do:

Read the books and discuss the history of aviation. Talk about the different forms of flying things. Share the pictures and figures. Allow the children to explore and play.

Have a baked potato bar for lunch today! Provide baked potatoes and all the fixings! Let the children choose butter, sour cream, cheese, bacon or salsa. Yum! Have the children come to school in bows. That could be bow ties, or hair bows or anything in between. If you happen to have a bow-tying dressing frame. Showcase it today. Have the children practice tying bows.

August 20

Celebration: World Mosquito Day

What You Will Need:
Books , pictures and figures of mosquitos

What You'll Do:
Read to the children about mosquitos, although they primarily seem to be pests, try to discuss their purpose and interesting facts. Share photos and any figures you may have found. You can also talk to the children about preventing mosquito bites today.

August 21

Celebration: Senior Citizens Day, Poet Day

What You Will Need:

Cards, treats, Poems

What You'll Do:

Have the children make cards or treats for senior citizens in a center or home near you. Respect for our eldest members of society is so important and young children recognize this. Allow them to shine today.

Gather a few favorite poems and share them with the children. Talk about the people who wrote them and what they may have been thinking about or feeling when the composed the poem. If you can, invite a local poet to visit your classroom.

August 22

Celebration: Be an Angel Day

What You Will Need:
Nothing!

What You'll Do:
Sometimes, we just need to take a step back and be of service to others. Today is the perfect day to show the children how to be someone's angel. You may have a need in your community or a family in your school that needs help. It could be as simple as assisting someone with the door, or helping the custodians by doing a few extra steps.

August 23

Celebration: Sponge Cake Day, Daffodil Day

What You Will Need:
Sponge cake, daffodils

What You'll Do:
Sponge cake today just use store-bought.
Have a few fresh daffodils that the children can arrange
and maybe have a fancy snack-time all together.
Maybe add a little tea or lemonade for a truly special
occasion!

August 24

Celebration: Peach Pie Day, International Strange Music Day, Knife Day

What You Will Need:

Peach pie, samples of international music, blunt tip knives
What You'll Do: Provide some peach pie for the children
to enjoy. Top it with ice cream for a really special treat.
We must be careful not to imply that we are making fun
of another country/culture's music. Perhaps just play a
few samples of international music and not label it as
"strange". You can find samples with unusual or
uncommon instruments or sounds. The children will enjoy
it for sure.

If you have a cooking area, you may want to introduce
blunt tipped knives. It may sound outrageous and you'll
have to check your regulations, but don't be scared .
Show the children how to use a knife properly. They will
surprise you! Start with something easy, like slicing a
banana and move to other foods. Small children cut best
when using a sawing motion.

You may want to skip Knife Day.

August 25

Theme: Banana Split Day

What You Will Need:

Supplies for banana splits- bananas, ice cream
(chocolate strawberry and vanilla) whipped cream,
cherries, chopped nuts (if possible).

What You'll Do:

Talk about the history of the Banana Split and variations
of it. Prepare the Banana Splits with the children, allow
them to help or scoop as much as possible. Enjoy!

August 26

Celebration: Dog Day

What You Will Need:
Books, photos, and figures of dogs

What You'll Do:
Read the books and share photos of different breeds of cats. You can also talk about any cats the children may have as pets.

August 27

Celebration: Banana Lovers Day

What You Will Need:
Bananas

What You'll Do:
There are so many things you could do today! Have the children "draw" or "write" on bananas with toothpicks in the morning. As the day goes on the writings and drawings will begin to appear. Enjoy the banana magic! Or, you could provide all kinds of foods made with bananas- pudding, bread, splits or smoothies.

August 28

Celebration: Bowtie Day, Cherry Turnover Day

What You Will Need:
Bowties, cherry turnovers

What You'll Do:
Have the children wear bowties to school or have a few on hand for the children to try on. Discuss the history of bowties and maybe mention a few famous bowtie wearing folks. If you want to be really creative, try some crafts using bowtie pasta or enjoy bowtie pasta for lunch. If you do have bowties for lunch, why not have a cherry popover for dessert. There are several easy recipes that children could navigate easily or have some premade.

Enjoy this fancy day!

August 29

Celebration: Lemon Juice Day

What You Will Need:
lemon juice

What You'll Do:
There are many uses for lemon juice. You could make lemonade with the children. You could write secret messages in lemon juice and show the children how to make them appear.

August 30

Celebration: Toasted Marshmallow Day, Slinky Day

What You Will Need:

Marshmallows, ways to toast them, Slinkies

What You'll Do:

Depending on what you have available to you, you can toast marshmallows with the children. Have a volunteer or two come by and help toast them on a small grill outdoors. Enjoy!

Provide a few Slinkies for the children to play with. Try them on the stairs, see how far they will go!

August 31

Celebration: Trail Mix Day

What You Will Need:

Trail mix ingredients (nuts, granola, dried fruit, small candy pieces)

What You'll Do:

Have the children choose their own ingredients to make the perfect trail mix. Head outside with the trail mix for a hike around the neighborhood or playground.

Consider choking hazards.

SEPTEMBER

SEPTEMBER

September 1

Celebration: Letter Writing Day, Tofu Day

What You Will Need:
Letter writing supplies, addresses, tofu

What You'll Do:
Children are excited about writing, so writing a letter should be part of the process! Explain to the children how to write a letter. Give them examples. It may be a several step process, but take it slow it will be worth it. Have them families send in addresses of relatives or have the children send "mail" to each other.

Tofu, what can we do with tofu? Almost anything. Talk with the children about tofu. Prepare some or have some prepared and share with the children.

Small children can use stamps and stickers as an adaptation.

September 2

Celebration: Blueberry Popsicle Day

What You Will Need:
Blueberries, popsicle molds, milk, or juice

What You'll Do:
Have the children mix blueberries and whatever drink you choose and pour them into molds, freeze for a few hours and enjoy!

September 3

Celebration: Skyscraper Day see August 10th

What You Will Need:
Books, photos and figures of skyscrapers

What You'll Do:
If you celebrated on August 10th you can expand on those discussions and activities. If you didn't get the chance, read books, share photos and discuss skyscrapers. Look and see what you may have on hand to build a few as a group.

September 4

Celebration: Macadamia Nut Day, Wildlife Day

What You Will Need:

Macadamia nuts, books, pictures and figures of wildlife

What You'll Do:

Provide the children with macadamia nuts to sample. Be mindful of nut allergies and choking hazards.

September 5

Celebration: Cheese Pizza Day, International Day of Charity, Be Late for Something Day

What You Will Need:
Cheese Pizza, a cause

What You'll Do:
Provide the all-time favorite cuisine of children….cheese pizza! Have a blast!

We are always looking for ways to help and today is no different. Use it as an example of being a charitable person. Find a local cause or one that means something to your classroom and do good deeds for them!

Be punctual is very important and something we try to teach the children each day. But, perhaps, today, if we were late a few times, we could show them the consequences of being tardy. Remember this may cause the flow of the day to go awry, so proceed with caution.

September 6

Celebration: Read a Book Day

What You Will Need:
Books

What You'll Do:
Pick a few of the class favorites and s t together and read them. Maybe head outside with a blanket and spend some time reading out there. Stress the importance of books and reading and have a good time.

September 7

Celebration: Acorn Squash Day, Salami Day

What You Will Need:
Acorn squash, salami

What You'll Do:
Have an acorn squash for the children to observe. You can cut it open and let them see inside. You could also have some prepared so they can taste it.

For Salami day, you want to have some salami cut with cheese and crackers. Children can sample it alone or with familiar favorites. Tasty!

September 8

Celebration: Literacy Day, Iguana Day

What You Will Need:
books, some about iguanas, photos and figures of
iguanas

What You'll Do:
Pick a few of the class favorites and sit together and
read them. Maybe head outside again with a blanket
and spend some time reading out there. Stress the
importance of literacy and reading and have a good
time.

Read to the children about iguanas. Share photos and
figures of iguanas and allow the children to explore and
play. If you have an iguana as a class pet, throw an
iguana party. If not, maybe invite one to come visit? The
children would love to observe a live iguana.

September 9

Celebration: Teddy Bear Day

What You Will Need:

Teddy bears

What You'll Do:

Ask the children to bring in their own teddy bear. Talk about the history of the teddy bear and introduce Teddy Roosevelt. You may want to put name tags on the teddy bears with the child's name as well to avoid mix-ups or lost bears.

September 10

Celebration: Alpaca Day, Swap Ideas Day

What You Will Need:

Books. Pictures and figures of alpacas

What You'll Do:

Read to the children about alpacas. Discuss their habitats and interesting facts. Allow the children to explore the pictures and play with the figures. If you can find a live alpaca in your area, think about inviting it to school! How fun!

We swap ideas each day in our classrooms. Emphasize this today and explain how important it is to the children's learning process. The children will feel even more a part of the community you are building.

September 11

Celebration: Hot Cross Buns Day, Make Your Bed Day

What You Will Need:

Hot Cross buns, the song

What You'll Do:

Prepare hot cross buns with the children. Teach them the song as you work. Discuss the history of hot cross buns. If you are unable to make them, use store-bought.

Talk with the children about making their bed each day. You can share the importance of starting the day off right or keeping their room tidy. We must not overstep our boundaries, as some parents don't require a made bed, but there is something really nice about coming home and the room is tidy and the bed is made.

September 12

Celebration: Chocolate Milkshake Day

What You Will Need:

Chocolate ice cream, milk, blender

What You'll Do:

Mix the ice cream and milk in the blender for a smooth treat. You can provide whipped cream and a cherry for the full effect.

September 13

Celebration: Roald Dahl Day, Fortune Cookie Day, Kids Take Over the Kitchen Day

What You Will Need:

Roald Dahl books, Fortune cookies, cooking projects and utensils

What You'll Do:

Introduce the children to the works od Roald Dahl. They may be familiar with some of the books already. Today would be a great day to start reading a chapter book by Dahl to the children.

Provide fortune cookies to the children. Share fortunes and discuss the history of fortune cookies.

You may have the ability to cook or prepare food in t=your classroom. If you do, have the children think of a dish, write the recipe and follow it. See how it turns out. If you don't, maybe let the children prepare a small dish. Do as much as you are able, allowing the children to take over as much as possible.

September 14

Celebration: Eat a Hoagie Day, Cream Filled Donut Day

What You Will Need:

Hoagies (lunch meats, cheeses, lettuce tomatoes, condiments , hoagie rolls) cream filled donuts

What You'll Do:

Have hoagies for lunch! Ask the children to help prepare their own hoagie. They should be able to assemble a sandwich. Help only if needed.

Cream filled donuts are dreamy, share a few with the children today. You could cut up a few and let the children try different flavors without eating a whole donut.

September 15

Celebration: Batman Day, International Red Panda Day, Linguine Day

What You Will Need:
Batman t-shirts/apparel, Books, pictures, and figures of Red Pandas

What You'll Do:
Have the children come to school wearing their finest Batman apparel.

Read the books and discuss the habitats and interesting facts about red pandas. Share the pictures and figures and allow the children to explore and play. Celebrate Linguine Day by preparing the pasta to eat with the children. You can provide a variety of sauces to go along with it.

You can also use uncooked linguine noodles to place into containers with narrow holes. Increase the difficulty as the children master each thing you give them.

September 16

Celebration: Play Doh Day, Cinnamon Raisin Bread Day, Guacamole Day, Collect Rocks Day

What You Will Need:

Play Doh, Cinnamon raisin bread, Guacamole, chips
Books or charts about rocks, small bag

What You'll Do:

Provide the children with several containers/colors of Play Doh. You can also provide tools roll, carve or imprint the Play Doh. Allow the children to create !
Today, you have two choices, both are yummy! Give the children the choice to make cinnamon raisin bread, or guacamole. Both can be made simply, you may need to bake the bread off-site. Or provide prepared treats for the children. Serve the guacamole with chips and the cinnamon raisin bread with a little butter. Yum!
Read over the books and harts and head outside to collect some rocks. See if you can identify them. Look for cool colors and shapes. Provide a small bag for the children to keep their collection in.

September 17

Celebration: Constitution Day, Apple Dumpling Day, International Country Music Day

What You Will Need:

A copy of the Constitution, Apple Dumplings, Samples of country music

What You'll Do:

Read over the Constitution with the children. Perhaps you could recite the Preamble. Discuss the history and significance of the Constitution.

Use prepared apple dumplings or a simple recipe you can prepare with the children. Enjoy with frozen yogurt or ice cream.

Share samples of country music with the children. Try a few from different eras. Discuss which ones the children like, some of the artists and the history of country music. You may just identify the Constitution.

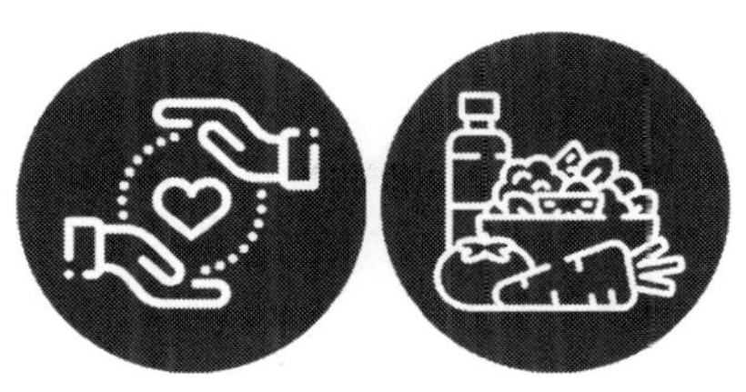

September 18

Celebration: Respect Day, Cheeseburger Day

What You Will Need:
Cheeseburgers

What You'll Do:
Talk with the children about respect. This can include for their teachers, their families, each other and respect for themselves. Role playing may help solidify this concept. Provide tiny sliders for the children to enjoy. Encourage them to try different condiments. Be mindful of dietary restrictions.

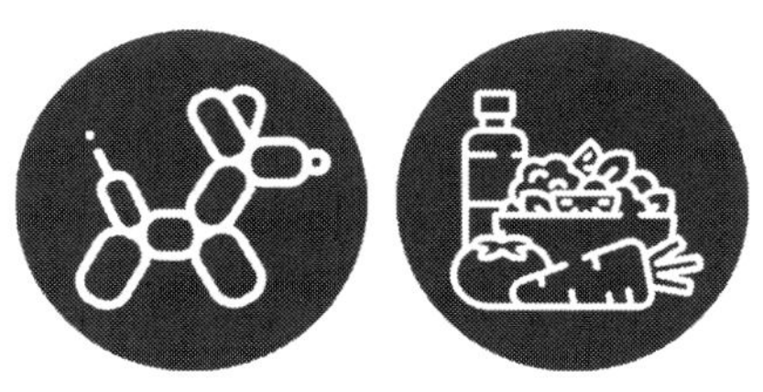

September 19

Celebration: Talk Like a Pirate Day, Butterscotch Pudding Day

What You Will Need:
Butterscotch pudding

What You'll Do:
Argh matey's! Talk like a Pirate Day might be one of the most well-known celebrations. This day is sure to be fun. Speak with the children just like Captain Hook! If your children are working on their phonograms- the "ar" sound would be a good one to emphasize today! Provide the children with butterscotch pudding today. You can make it in the classroom, or buy snack-packs.

The children will be delighted!

September 20

Celebration: Pepperoni Pizza Day, Punch Day

What You Will Need:
Pepperoni pizza, punch

What You'll Do:
This sounds like the makings of a Pizza Party! Serve pepperoni pizza an punch and celebrate two days at once!

September 21

Celebration: Miniature Golf Day, World Gratitude Day, International Day of Peace

What You Will Need:
Mini golf clubs, golf balls, mini golf sets

What You'll Do:
Set up a small mini golf course using what you were able to obtain. Make it more challenging as you go. International Day of Peace and World Gratitude Day go hand in hand. Consider creating a peace table or having the children write in gratitude journals. There are so many possibilities, follow the children' lead. These are two days that we must emphasize with the children. The world can be unkind and unfair, so incorporating these concepts is imperative to our work with the children.

September 22

**Celebration: Doodle Day, World Rhino Day,
Ice Cream Cone Day**

What You Will Need:

Paper and pencils, Books, pictures and figures of rhinos,
Ice cream cones

What You'll Do:

Provide paper and pencils so that the children may
doodle. Provide examples of fun doodles and let the
children explore.

Read books, and discuss fun facts about rhinos. Share the
photos and figures with the children and allow them to
explore and play.

Provide ice cream cones for the children. You can either
provide ice cream and scoops or a prepackaged cone
will do.

September 23

Celebration: Checkers Day

What You Will Need:
Checkers and a checkboard

What You'll Do:
Teach the children the game of checkers. Have a few boards going at the same time. Help the children as the learn how to play.

September 24

Celebration: Punctuation Day

What You Will Need:
Sample text, examples of each symbol.

What You'll Do:
Show the children the sample texts with plenty of examples of punctuation symbols. Show them the examples of each symbol and see if they can find a few. Talk about what each one means. This is a big concept for young children, so treat this an introductory lesson.

Name the symbols with the children

September 25

Celebration: Dream Day

What You Will Need:

Dream interpretation books

What You'll Do:

Talk to the children about dreams. This could be nighttime dreams, day dreams or hope and dreams. If you want to talk about night time dreams you could share a few interpretations with the children.

September 26

Celebration: Fitness Day

What You Will Need:
fitness equipment

What You'll Do:
Have the children come to school wearing appropriate clothes and shoes. Talk about the importance of physical fitness. Demonstrate a few stretches and exercises (toe-touches, jumping jacks, etc.) If you have access to a gymnasium or fitness equipment. Use it. Jump ropes and hula hoops would work. You could also go for a long walk, or walk/run laps around the playground. Use what you have and adapt it to your setting.

September 27

Celebration: Fall Leaves

What You Will Need:
Nothing!

What You'll Do:
Head outside to check out the leaves. Discuss why the leaves are changing. Introduce fall songs about falling leaves.

September 28

Celebration: Good Neighbor Day

What You Will Need:
Nothing!

What You'll Do:
If your school is near a neighbor, you could plan something for them. If it's a business, think of how you could be a could neighbor to them. Your location will dictate how you celebrate. Remember that no matter how what you decide, remember that teaching the children the concept of being a good neighbor is the most important thing!

September 29

Celebration: Biscotti Day

What You Will Need:
Biscotti

What You'll Do:
Provide the children with biscotti. Use store bought biscotti. You can talk about where they originate from and what else is typically served with them.

September 30

Celebration: Rumi Day

What You Will Need:

Rumi quotes

What You'll Do:

Introduce the children to the wisdom of Rumi. Have a few quotes that you could have the children memorize, practice writing, or use at the peace table. Talk about Rumi and share interesting facts about him and his life.

OCTOBER

OCTOBER

October 1

Celebration: National Hair Day, National Homemade Cookies Day

What You Will Need:
Brushes or combs, cookies

What You'll Do:
Talk to the children about caring for their hair. You could ask them to bring in a hair brush or comb or provide one for each child. If you can obtain parent permission, you can style the children's hair and show them how to do it on their own. Or style the children's hair in funny styles. Make cookies in the classroom or have the children bring in their favorite homemade cookie. Have a taste-testing party or vote on the best one.

October 2

Celebration: National Custodial Workers Day, National Walk to School Day, Pumpkin Seed Day

What You Will Need:
Thank you notes, treats, Pumpkin Seeds

What You'll Do:
Talk with the children about the important work the custodians at school do. Make cards and treat in appreciation of them.

Talk to the parents and encourage them to walk to school, if possible.

Have pumpkin seeds on hand. You could roast them with the children or serve prepared seeds. You could also plant a pumpkin seed with the children and watch them grow!

Small children can use stamps and stickers as an adaptation.

October 3

Celebration: Hay Day

What You Will Need:

Hay

What You'll Do:

Gather as many bales of hay as you can and have the children climb, build and imagine with them. Hay makes a great backdrop for pictures, so this is a great time to snap some cute pics. Share with parents or save them for a special occasion.

October 4

Celebration: National Taco Day

What You Will Need:
Tacos and all the fixings

What You'll Do:
Make tacos with the children, provide all kinds of toppings and let the children build their own. Vote on which is better- hard or soft shells.

October 5

Celebration: Do Something Nice Day

What You Will Need:

A few nice projects

What You'll Do:

Consider the needs in your community. Discuss the possibilities with the children. We must teach the children the importance of being kind and doing good deeds, so including them in the discussions and decision making is very important. Do the good deeds you decide on and throw a few spontaneous ones in for good measure (hold the door for someone, offer assistance to someone carrying something). Gently point them out, so the children will notice, but so much that it's bragging. Small children can use stamps and stickers as an adaptation.

October 6

Celebration: National Mad Hatter's Day, National Noodle Day

What You Will Need:
A collection of hats, noodles

What You'll Do:
Have the children wear crazy hats to school or provide a few for them. You could have a "tea party" at snack time. You could also read a few sections from *Alice in Wonderland* that feature the mad hatter. Just remember to have fun with it!

You can have oodles of noodles today! You can make noodles and serve them with a variety of sauces. You could prepare several shapes/kinds of noodles and discuss the differences. You could use different shapes of uncooked noodles to create a group art project. If you've been doing a lot of cooking, this may be nice change.

October 7

Celebration: Chocolate Covered Pretzel Day, Child Health Day

What You Will Need:

Chocolate covered pretzels, health info for parents

What You'll Do:

You can serve prepared pretzels or have the children cover their own in chocolate. Yum!

Most days we educate the children. While you can discuss health topics with the children today, it is important to share information with the parents. Gather some health information for parents and send it home in honor of Child Health Day. Topics could include- dental info, how old a child should be for their first visit, how to brush teeth properly and teach children to begin to brush their own teeth. You could also include a list of local dentists or clinics. Health info- this could include info on sleep, nutrition, screen time, ADD/ADHD or autism checklist or information, and maybe exercise/outdoor time info. Think about the needs of your families. Parents can be so busy and overwhelmed and will appreciate the time and care we put into helping them.

Adapt info for parents to this age group.

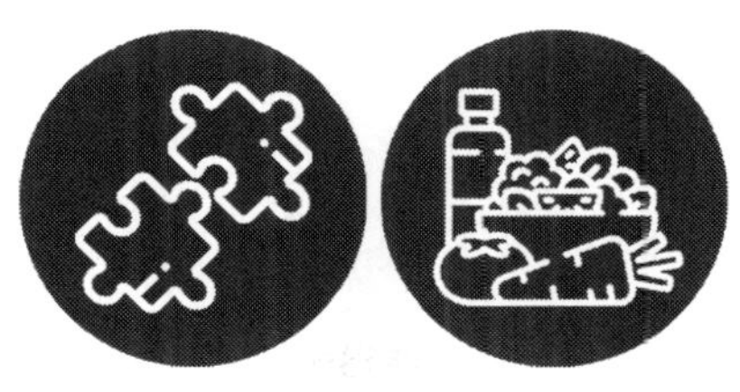

October 8

Celebration: Touch Tag Day, Fluffernutter Day

What You Will Need:
peanut butter, marshmallow cream, bread

What You'll Do:
Tag! You're it! Get out for a rousing game of tag today!

Follow up with a yummy Fluffernutter sandwich. Have the children make peanut butter and marshmallow cream sandwiches to satisfy the appetite they worked up playing tag. Be mindful of allergies.

October 9

Celebration: Bring Your Teddy Bear to School Day, Stop Bullying Day

What You Will Need:

Teddy Bears

What You'll Do:

Have the children bring their teddy bears to school today for an extra element of fun. Sing teddy songs and discuss the history of the teddy bear.

The topic of bullying can be tricky in the early childhood community. We must be careful not to label any child a "bully" when they are still learning and refining social skills. Still, there is a lot we can do to help deter "bully" behavior. Giving some examples or role-playing, will help children relate to and recognize behaviors that are not socially acceptable.

October 10

Celebration: Angel Food Cake Day, World Mental Health Day

What You Will Need:
Angel Food Cake, Pediatric Mental Health information

What You'll Do:
Serve angel food cake today and watch the smiles multiply!

You can gather info for parents about pediatric mental health. For the children, you could discuss emotions, how to handle sadness or anger, and peaceful activities to promote mental wellness.

Adapt parent info for this age group.

October 11

Celebration: Sausage Pizza Day

What You Will Need:

Sausage Pizza

What You'll Do:

Serve this childhood favorite today and you'll be a hero for sure! You can make them with the children or have them delivered. Either way, it's going to be a great day!

October 12

Celebration: Costume Swap Day,
I Love Yarn Day

What You Will Need:
Costumes, yarn

What You'll Do:
Have the children bring or wear costumes. Swap them and have a big costume party!

Break out the yarn today, create accessories for the costumes, teach the children how to braid, or finger knit. Have fun!

October 13

Celebration: Autumn Leaves Day

What You Will Need:
Fall leaves

What You'll Do:
Head outside to play in the leaves. Try to catch falling leaves, rake piles for jumping or create some outdoor natural art. Sing songs about falling leaves or color/paint fall scenes.

October 14

Celebration: Dessert Day

What You Will Need:
Desserts

What You'll Do:
Have a dessert party! Ask each child to bring a dessert to sample. You can challenge families to find healthy dessert options to help cut down on the sugar intake.

October 15

Celebration: Cheese Curd Day, Grouch Day

What You Will Need:
Cheese Curds

What You'll Do:
Provide cheese curds for the children to sample. Making your own would probably be a bit much for the classroom.

We have all been a bit grouchy. Help the children recognize grouchy feelings and talk about ways to cheer up and what can lead to grouchy feelings
(not eating, lack of sleep, etc.)

October 16

Celebration: Dictionary Day, Take Your Parents to Lunch Day, Fossil Day

What You Will Need:
Dictionaries, Books, pictures and examples of fossils

What You'll Do:
Introduce the children to the dictionary, explain the various parts, alphabetical order and if they are ready, parts of speech. Children love words and are excited about reading, so encourage the use of the dictionary.

They could practice writing or spelling words they find. Invite parents to eat with the children today. Have the children prepare name cards, set the table or arrange some flowers in preparation of their parents arrival. Read to the children about fossils, discuss interesting facts. Share pictures and examples of fossils. Head outside for a fossil hunt!

Remember, it may be upsetting for this age group to see their parents and then have them leave. This may be an activity to skip if your class isn't settled.

October 17

Celebration: Pasta Day

What You Will Need:
Pasta

What You'll Do:
Similar to October 6th, you have a lot of options today. You can make pasta and serve it with a variety of sauces. You could prepare several shapes/kinds of pasta and discuss the differences. You could use different shapes of uncooked pasta to create a group art project. If you've been doing a lot of cooking, this may be nice change. If you celebrated on the 6th, build on those experiences or go a completely different way. Follow the interests of the children.

October 18

Celebration: Chocolate Cupcake Day

What You Will Need:

Chocolate cupcakes

What You'll Do:

Make or buy chocolate cupcakes for the children. You could use a recipe that "hides" vegetables to cut down on sugar intake.

October 19

Celebration: New Friends Day

What You Will Need:
Nothing

What You'll Do:
Encourage the children to make new fr ends. Be careful, small children consider all their classmates friends. We must watch our phrasing. Encourage friendships in the classroom. You could also have them make a friend in another classroom or consider pen pals?

October 20

Celebration: Sloth Day

What You Will Need:
Books, pictures and figures of sloths

What You'll Do:
Read to the children about sloths. Discuss their habitats, needs and interesting facts. Share photos and figures for the children to investigate.

October 21

Celebration: Pumpkin Cheesecake Day, Reptile Awareness Day

What You Will Need:

Pumpkin Cheesecake, Books, picture and figure of reptiles

What You'll Do:

Serve pumpkin cheesecake bites to the children in celebration of pumpkin season!

Read to the children about reptiles, their characteristics and discuss any interesting facts you may discover. Share pictures and figure and allow the children explore.

October 22

Celebration: Nut Day, Color Day

What You Will Need:
A Variety of Nuts (Be mindful of allergies), Watercolors

What You'll Do:
If you are able to celebrate, collect a variety of nuts. Have the children identify and sort them. They could also sample them. If you can't use actual nuts- photos may be a nice substitution.

Provide watercolors and paper and talk to the children about colors and how to create shades and hues. Have to children practice color mixing.

October 23

Celebration: Boston Cream Pie

What You Will Need:

Boston Cream Pie

What You'll Do:

Have the children sample this delicious dish. Talk about the origin of the dessert and how it got its name.

October 24

Celebration: Food Day, United Nations Day

What You Will Need:
Food drive, UN info

What You'll Do:
We cook and eat a lot of food in the early childhood classrooms. Today, in honor of National Food Day, maybe we could remember those who may not be able to celebrate. Ask the children to bring in food to share with the local food bank or other charity in need.

Discuss what the UN is and does. Even though we work with young children, they can and should be aware of the world around them- they will be running it soon enough! Read over the United Nations Bill of Rights or the Universal Declaration of Human Rights. You don't have to read each one, but a great discussion could emerge, so encourage the children to contribute today.

October 25

Celebration: Breadstick Day

What You Will Need:

Breadsticks

What You'll Do:

Make breadsticks with the children in your classroom or provide prepared ones. You can serve them with a variety of dipping sauces to make it more interesting.

October 26

Celebration: Mule Day, Pumpkin Day

What You Will Need:
Books, pictures and figures of mules, pumpkins or field trip to a pumpkin patch

What You'll Do:
Read to the children about mules and their historical significance. Discuss interesting facts and share photos or figures with the children.

If you can, head out on a field trip to a pumpkin patch so the children can pick a pumpkin. If that's not possible, provide pumpkins for the children to paint. Talk about the life cycle of the pumpkin and favorite pumpkin uses.

October 27

Celebration: Black Cat Day

What You Will Need:

Photos of black cats, songs

What You'll Do:

Talk to the children about black cats. We must remember not to perpetuate stigmas or superstitions. Sing songs or recite poems about black cats.

October 28

Celebration: Chocolate Day

What You Will Need:

Chocolate

What You'll Do:

Just before Halloween! Share a tiny piece of chocolate with the children at snack or lunch time. Mix it up and try dark or white chocolate.

October 29

Celebration: Oatmeal Day

What You Will Need:
Oatmeal and all the fixings

What You'll Do:
Create an oatmeal bar, provide all kinds of fruit and nuts, and other toppings for the children to sample and create oatmeal perfection.

October 30

Celebration: Candy Corn Day

What You Will Need:

Candy Corn

What You'll Do:

Love it or hate it, it's that time of year to eat candy corn. Share a few pieces with the children and enjoy a sweet treat!

October 31

Celebration: Caramel Day

What You Will Need:
Caramels

What You'll Do:
While you may be celebrating Halloween today, you could choose to taste caramels with the children today. If you do, add a bit of history in there, too!

NOVEMBER

NOVEMBER

November 1

Celebration: Author's Day, Family Literacy Day

What You Will Need:
Collection of books

What You'll Do:
Gather the children and talk about author's and what they do. Discuss some of your class' favorite books and who the author's are. You could also talk about famous author's and share a few passages from their works. Share with families some literature on literacy. You may have families that need help reading, so sharing resources that will help them is very important. You could also send home info on the importance of early literacy or local library info.

November 2

Celebration: Bison Day

What You Will Need:
Books, phots and figures of bison

What You'll Do:
Read to the children about bison and their historical significance. Share and discuss interesting facts you may discover. Allow the children to explore the photos and figures.

November 3

Celebration: Sandwich Day

What You Will Need:
bread, lunch meats, cheeses, nut butters, jellies, condiments

What You'll Do:
Provide a build your own sandwich station for the children. (Cut the bread into small pieces so the children can sample more than one if they choose.)

November 4

Celebration: Candy Day

What You Will Need:
Candy

What You'll Do:
Even though you may never want to see another piece of candy again, today is a day to celebrate it. Think of alternate uses for the candy, maybe collect it and donate it? Or make an art project? Get creative as you get rid of it.

November 5

Celebration: Doughnut Day

What You Will Need:
Doughnuts

What You'll Do:
Here's another day that you may want to get a bit creative. While you could provide doughnuts for the children, maybe today you could paint a picture of doughnuts? We all love doughnuts, but the timing of this day is a bit too much. Perhaps you could ask a local doughnut shop to provide coupons for free doughnuts and give them to the children as prizes for running "doughnuts" outside. They could redeem the doughnut another day.

November 6

Celebration: Nachos Day, Saxophone Day

What You Will Need:

nachos and all the fixings, samples of music featuring the saxophone, picture of the saxophone and if possible a real saxophone and/or musician

What You'll Do:

Provide a nacho bar and have the children build their own, encouraging them to try new things they may not have tried before.

Play samples of saxophones for the children, show them pictures of saxophones, name the anatomy of the saxophone. If possible invite a musician to come and play for the children.

November 7

Celebration: Stress Awareness Day

What You Will Need:
Stress balls, fidget activities

What You'll Do:
Talk with the children about stress. Explain what it feels like. Talk to the children about healthy and appropriate way to deal with those feelings. Introduce stress balls and other items you may have to help deal with stress.

November 8

Celebration: Parents as Teachers Day

What You Will Need:
Personal letters from you

What You'll Do:
We must always acknowledge the child's first teacher-the parents (or guardians). Write a personal letter to each family acknowledging something lovely you've noticed about their child and how much their child learns from them. It's an amazing way to build the bond between parent and teacher.

November 9

Celebration: World Freedom Day

What You Will Need:
Nothing

What You'll Do:
Today, we celebrate the fall of the Berlin Wall. This is a pretty heavy subject, so focus on the freedoms we human should expect. Talk about why they are important. Encourage a discussion.

November 10

Celebration: Vanilla Cupcake Day

What You Will Need:

Vanilla cupcakes

What You'll Do:

Serve the children vanilla cupcakes. You can use a recipe that incorporates fruits or veggies to cut down on the sugars.

November 11

Celebration: Veteran's Day

What You Will Need:

Needs of veterans

What You'll Do:

Contact your local veteran's agency and determine what needs the veterans in your area have. It could be notes and cards from the children, care packages or other donations. Once you know, set out to meet that need with the children. Talk about veteran's and the value of their service. Incorporate their ideas as much as possible.

Small children can use stamps and stickers as an adaptation.

November 12

Celebration: Model Train Day

What You Will Need:
Model Trains

What You'll Do:
November is National Model Railroad Month. Invite
local train enthusiasts to class to share their trains
and talk to the children.

You can read stories about trains and their history
ahead of time. You could also provide picture cards
of several different trains for the
children to identify.

Infant/Toddler Adaptation:
Use this opportunity to name objects, parts of the trains,
tracks, conductor, etc.

November 13

Celebration: World Kindness Day, Educational Support Professionals Day

What You Will Need:
Thank you note from you

What You'll Do:
Be kind today! Discuss the importance of kindness and emphasize some kind things you may notice today. If you happen to have an Educational Support Professional in your classroom or school, write a thank you note and perhaps include a small treat to acknowledge your appreciation for all they do. Small children can use stamps and stickers as an adaptation.

November 14

Celebration: Pickle Day

What You Will Need:
A variety of pickles

What You'll Do:
Provide a variety of pickles for the children to sample. Talk about the different tastes and how pickles are made.

November 15

Celebration: America Recycles Day

What You Will Need:
Recycling container, books or info about recycling

What You'll Do:
Talk to the children about recycling and its importance. If you don't already have one, provide a recycling container and explain what materials can go in it.

November 16

Celebration: Button Day

What You Will Need:
Buttons, sewing materials, art materials

What You'll Do:
If you can, each the children how to sew a button. If that's not possible, provide art supplies that the children can use to create art projects with the buttons.

November 17

Celebration: Take a Hike Day, Homemade Bread Day

What You Will Need:

Permission from parents, ingredients to make homemade bread

What You'll Do:

If you are lucky enough to be near a fun hiking spot, try to get out and go for a short hike. If not, "hike" around the neighborhood or even the playground.
If possible, prepare homemade bread with the children, if not provide prepared homemade bread for the children. You can discuss the process of making bread from wheat to table.

November 18

Celebration: Mickey Mouse Birthday

What You Will Need:

Mickey themed clothing, cake or cupcakes

What You'll Do:

Celebrate the mouse's birthday by having the children come to school wearing any Mickey memorabilia they may have. Provide cupcakes or cake with ears. Enjoy!

November 19

Celebration: World Toilet Day

What You Will Need:
Books about toilets, photos of toilets around the world

What You'll Do:
Talk with the children about toilets. Explain how they work, use this opportunity to go over proper usage, or talk about different "toilets" around the world. It may not be the most appealing day, but children are genuinely interested. Try to meet their interest.

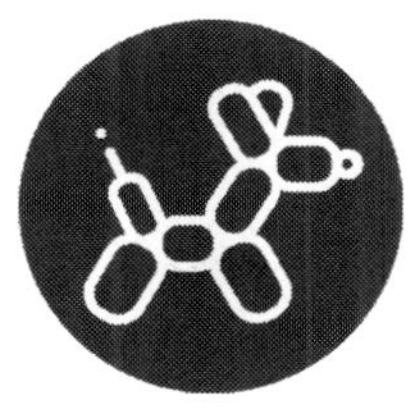

November 20

Celebration: Absurdity Day

What You Will Need:

Photos of absurd things

What You'll Do:

Children love funny, unusual things. Start by explaining what absurdity means. The word itself will delight the children. Share with them some absurd photos you found. Discuss. Share stories.

This concept may be lost on this age group. Share anyway.

November 21

Celebration: Gingerbread Cookie Day

What You Will Need:

Gingerbread cookies (ingredients or store bought) icing, candies or raisins

What You'll Do:

Make gingerbread cookies with the children, if it's not possible provide them. Have the children decorate the cookies using icing and candies or raisins.

November 22

Celebration: Cranberry Relish Day

What You Will Need:

Cranberry relish

What You'll Do:

You could find a simple recipe to make a cranberry relish or provide some for the children. Talk about cranberries and their significance this time of year.

November 23

Celebration: Cashew Day

What You Will Need:
Cashews (if possible, be mindful of allergies)

What You'll Do:
Provide cashews for the children to sample. Talk about where they come from , how they grow and what their shell looks like.

November 24

Celebration: Sardine Day

What You Will Need:
Sardines (maybe crackers or melba toast)

What You'll Do:
Provide sardines for the children to sample. If this doesn't seem like something that work in your classroom, you could talk about where sardines live, their habitats and interesting facts.

November 25

Celebration: Parfait Day

What You Will Need:

Parfait ingredients

What You'll Do:

Find a simple recipe that works for your group of children and prepare parfaits. Enjoy this delicious French dessert!

November 26

Celebration: Cake Day

What You Will Need:

Cake ingredients

What You'll Do:

Discuss cakes and how to make them. Talk about different recipes and have the children decide on a fun cake to try to make. Gather the ingredients and get started. If making a cake isn't possible, think about providing one that the children make not have tried before.

November 27

Celebration: Juke Box Day

What You Will Need:

Pictures or short videos of Juke Boxes, if you have access to one (table top) bring it in.

What You'll Do:

If you cannot have the real thing show the children how the juke box works and make your own! Create the façade of a juke box and have the children "choose" songs. Play them using a digital device.

November 28

Celebration: French Toast Day

What You Will Need:

Bread, eggs, milk and cinnamon or premade French toast.

What You'll Do:

If you can make French toast, prepare it with the children. If that's not possible, provide French toast or French toast sticks and fruit and syrup for a yummy treat!

November 29

Celebration: Flossing Day

What You Will Need:
Floss (teeth model if available)

What You'll Do:
Discuss with the children the importance of oral hygiene. Demonstrate how to floss and allow the children a chance to try themselves. Maintain hygienic practices for this activity.

Perhaps flossing a model would work best.

November 30

Celebration: Mason Jar Day

What You Will Need:

Mason Jars

What You'll Do:

There are more things to do with mason jars than there are days of the year. Think about what you have on hand and what you need to accomplish for your room. Maybe a holiday craft? Maybe planters or vases? Maybe gifts for the upcoming holidays? Or a savings jar? So many possibilities!

DECEMBER

DECEMBER

December 1

Celebration: Eat a Red Apple Day, Rosa Parks Day

What You Will Need:

Red apples, Books and photos of Rosa Parks
What You'll Do: Provide red apples for the children to eat for a snack or at lunch.

Read to the children about Rosa Parks and her contributions to history. Share photos of her.

December 2

Celebration: Fritters Day, Special Education Day

What You Will Need:
Fritters, Thank you notes

What You'll Do:
Provide the children with fritters to sample. This may be too intensive to make in the classroom.
If you work with any Special Educators, take a moment to recognize the work they do. Thank you notes or a lovely treat goes a long way and we must support each other!

Small children can use stamps and stickers as an adaptation.

December 3

Celebration: Trick Shot Day

What You Will Need:

Globetrotter videos, small basketball hoop, basketballs

What You'll Do:

Talk to the children about the Harlem Globetrotters and their trick shots. Watch a few video clips. Set up the child size hoop and have the children attempt a few shots.

December 4

Celebration: Cookie Day, Sock Day, Dice Day

What You Will Need:
Cookies, Socks, Dice

What You'll Do:
Provide cookies for the children, use a healthy recipe or healthy prepared cookie.

It's Sock Day- there are a lot of options today. You could have the children wear crazy socks to school. You could make sock puppets and put on a puppet show. If you are feeling adventurous you could make snowmen out of white socks. (There are some tutorials that require sewing and some that use rubber bands. So, look for what you think may work).

For Dice Day, you could have the children roll the dice and add up the numbers. You could also get creative and make your own board game. Or- go all out and make large dice and head outside for a life-size game. How fun!

December 5

Celebration: Bingo Day

What You Will Need:
Bingo Cards (numbers or pictures)

What You'll Do:
Explain the game of Bingo. Help the children grasp the concept. It may take a few tries, but it should be lots of fun!

Infant/Toddler Adaptation:
Children can find pictures and mark them. They may enjoy a stamper.

December 6

Celebration: St. Nicholas Day

What You Will Need:
Books and pictures of St. Nicholas

What You'll Do:
Approach this from a historical prospective, giving children the history behind St. Nicholas and the things they may be seeing this time of year associated with him. Discuss interesting facts and customs. Share the pictures with the children.

December 7

Celebration: Cotton Candy Day

What You Will Need:

Cotton Candy

What You'll Do:

If possible, have a cotton candy machine come to school so the children can see how it's made. If not, provide prepared cotton candy for the children to sample. You can talk about how it's made, how it became popular and any other interesting facts.

December 8

Celebration: Brownie Day, Pretend to be a Time Traveler Day

What You Will Need:
Brownies, Historical props

What You'll Do:
Provide the children with brownies for a yummy treat today. You can make them or use store bought. For time traveling, think about any items you may already have or have access to. Gather the children and travel through time. You can share the items and talk about what life may have been like in that time. Think about clothing, foods, technology/communication, and buildings/shelter. You can use short video clips or photos/pictures, too. Bring your brownies on your time traveling trip, you're sure to work up an appetite.

December 9

Celebration: Pastry Day

What You Will Need:

Pastries

What You'll Do:

Have the children bring in a variety of their favorite pastries to try new undiscovered delights. You could also focus on international pastries if you're feeling like a real treat!

December 10

Celebration: Human Rights Day, Nobel Peace Prize Day

What You Will Need:
Books or info about human rights (see October 24) and the Nobel Peace Prize

What You'll Do:
Discuss human rights. Even though we work with young children, they can and should be aware of the world around them- they will be running it soon enough! Read over the United Nations Bill of Rights or the Universal Declaration of Human Rights. You don't have to read each one, but a great discussion could emerge, so encourage the children to contribute today.
Explain what the Nobel Peace Prize is and discuss some of the winners and their accomplishments. Encourage the children to be like these leaders in their daily lives.

December 11

Celebration: Noodle Ring Day

What You Will Need:

Noodles in the shape of rings

What You'll Do:

Provide the children with noodle rings. Spaghetti- O's or a similar product may be just the way to celebrate.

December 12

Celebration: Gingerbread Day

What You Will Need:
Gingerbread, pre-made or the ingredients to make it

What You'll Do:
Prepare gingerbread or provide it for the children. You can use cookie cutters to make gingerbread people or a kit to make gingerbread houses. Instead of candy, try dried fruits to make a heathier choice when it comes to decorating your creations.

December 13

Celebration: Cocoa Day, Violin Day

What You Will Need:
Cocoa and samples of violin music

What You'll Do:
Provide the children with hot cocoa. Be mindful of the temperature. You can use a mix or prepare it from scratch with the children. Marshmallows or whipped cream would make this day even better!

For Violin Day, provide the children with sample of violin music. If possible, have a violinist come play for the children or provide a violin for the children to observe. Name the parts of the violin for them and encourage them to use the proper terminology.

December 14

Celebration: Monkey Day

What You Will Need:

Books, pictures, and figures of monkeys

What You'll Do:

Read to the children about monkeys, their habitats, diets and interesting facts. Share pictures and figures for the children to explore. You can talk about the many types of monkeys, the difference between monkeys and apes, and similarities and differences between monkeys and humans. Head outside and find some monkey bars or play monkey in the middle.

There are many songs and games about monkeys, select a few and have a blast!

December 15

Celebration: Lemon Cupcake Day, Bill of Rights Day

What You Will Need:

Lemon Cupcakes, Books, short videos about, and a copy of the Bill of Rights

What You'll Do:

Provide Lemon Cupcakes for the children. Have a perfectly sweet and sour day!

Read to the children about the Bill of Rights. Young children are not too young to get a few introductory lessons. Explain what the Bill of Rights are, give a general idea. There are great short videos for children, so if video is something you use, pick a short and simple one. Provide and copy of the Bill of Rights for the children to see.

December 16

Celebration: Chocolate Covered Anything Day

What You Will Need:
Melted chocolate and fruit

What You'll Do:
Provide the children with melted chocolate and fruits and have the children dip away. If you don't have fruit, maybe marshmallows or other delicious choices you may have on hand.

December 17

Celebration: Wright Brothers Day

What You Will Need:
Books, videos, photos and figures of the Wright Brothers or early planes

What You'll Do:
Share with the children stories of the Wright Brothers. Share videos, photos and figures for the children to explore. Make paper airplanes for the children to try to fly.

December 18

Celebration: Happy Holidays Day

What You Will Need:
Books, photos and props for all of the winter holidays

What You'll Do:
Talk to the children about the holidays that occur during this time of year. Read books, share photos and encourage families to come in and talk about the way their families celebrate various holiday. Be respectful and have a blast!

December 19

Celebration: Oatmeal Muffin Day

What You Will Need:
Oatmeal Muffins

What You'll Do:
Make oatmeal muffins with the children. There may even be a few no-bake options you could explore if baking isn't an option in your classroom. Enjoy your healthy treats!

December 20

Celebration: Ugly Christmas Sweater Day

What You Will Need:
Christmas Sweaters

What You'll Do:
Have the children come dressed in their Christmas sweaters. Be mindful that small children don't think of "ugly" things as ugly. They may love the tacky tassels or dancing Christmas unicorns. So, perhaps drop the "ugly" and just have fun in some wild Christmas gear!

December 21

Celebration: National Flashlight Day

What You Will Need:
Flashlights

What You'll Do:
Have the children bring in flashlights and provide a few, too. Darken your room or go to a dark space and have a flashlight party. You can play games- like hide a few objects around the room mostly in plain sight, have the children shine their lights until they find them. Have the children shine their lights to make shapes or "write" letters. Use your imagination, follow the children's lead.

Have some fun!

(There is a great Louis Armstrong song- Zat you Santa Claus that would be super cute if you hide a Santa for the children to find. Check it out and see if it would work in your classroom).

December 22

Celebration: Date Nut Bread Day

What You Will Need:
Date Nut Bread

What You'll Do:
Make or provide date nut bread with the children.
Perhaps adapt the recipe to eliminate the nuts.

December 23

Celebration: Roots Day, Forefathers Day

What You Will Need:
Books about ancestry, globe, info about the children

What You'll Do:
This day can be a bit tricky to navigate, some children will not know their history. So, maybe share yours or discuss the various ways all of the people came to live in America. Young children are still very innocent, so being truthful, yet appropriate is imperative. We must educate, yet try not to crush their hopeful spirits. It's a fine line, so prepare and give as much information as you think appropriate for your group.

If you are able to get countries of origin for the children, have a globe and locate the countries with the children.

December 24

Celebration: Eggnog Day

What You Will Need:
Eggnog

What You'll Do:
Provide eggnog for the children to sample. Talk about the history and traditions of eggnog.

December 25

Celebration: Pumpkin Pie Day

What You Will Need:

Pumpkin Pie

What You'll Do:

Provide or make pumpkin pie with the children. Pumpkin pie is such a traditional favorite! Talk about the history and traditions associated with the holidays and pumpkin pie.

December 26

Celebration: Candy Cane Day

What You Will Need:
Candy Canes

What You'll Do:
Give the children candy canes. There are so many varieties now, share them all. Talk about the history and traditions associated with the holidays and candy canes. Enjoy!

December 27

Celebration: Fruitcake Day

What You Will Need:
Fruitcake

What You'll Do:
Provide fruitcake for the children to sample. Talk about the history and traditions associated with the holidays and fruitcake.

December 28

Celebration: Christmas Candy Day

What You Will Need:
Christmas Candy

What You'll Do:
What to do with all of the leftover Christmas candy? Have the children bring it in for a swap. Or decorate any leftover Gingerbread houses or people with. Or collect it and make gift baskets for community workers or people in nursing homes.

December 29

Celebration: Tick Tock Day

What You Will Need:
Nothing

What You'll Do:
Today is a day of reflection. It's also a day to do anything you wanted to do this year, but haven't gotten to. Maybe there was day you didn't get to celebrate, or maybe the children want to do something again.

December 30

Celebration: Bacon Day

What You Will Need:
Bacon

What You'll Do:
Provide bacon for the children to sample. Pair it with eggs and pancakes and have breakfast for lunch.

December 31

Celebration: New Year's Eve

What You Will Need:

New Year's horns, hats, tiaras etc

What You'll Do:

Host a New Year's Celebration for the children. Talk about the symbols and traditions they may see or hear. Have a "countdown" along with time zones that are celebrating ahead of you.